Dreams Of Death

A Story of Mental Illness

I0118154

Lynda Anning

chipmunkapublishing
the mental health publisher

Published by
Chipmunkapublishing
United Kingdom

http://www.chipmunkapublishing.com

Copyright © Lynda Anning 2014

ISBN   978-1-78382-051-1

Chipmunkapublishing gratefully acknowledge the support of Arts Council England.

DEDICATION

To Mark, Dr. Peter Hughes, Chris, Bob, Dr.David Robertson, Michael
McKinnon, Nigel Munn, and all my loved ones.
For caring.

Dreams Of Death

Author Biography

Lynda Anning was born in Leith, near Edinburgh, Scotland in 1961; one of twin girls born to Maureen a twenty-two year old single mother. Lynda lived with her mother for a while but Maureen couldn't cope and the twins were fostered in Scotland and then sent to a Baptist Children's Home in Birchington, Kent. When they were three and a half years old they were adopted by a couple who lived in Essex.

Lynda experienced auditory hallucinations, trances and sleep problems as far back as she can remember. She was desperately unhappy throughout childhood and made her first suicide attempts at the age of six; trying to suffocate herself first with pillows and then with plastic bags. She told no-one.

She did well at primary school and passed the eleven plus and went to Grammar School. However, she struggled with depression, memory problems and social anxiety and was miserable at secondary school.

When she was fourteen her adoptive father died of cancer and later that year she was referred to a child psychiatrist at a child guidance clinic because she was stealing and underachieving at school. The psychiatrist diagnosed her with depression and she was offered appointments with a child psychotherapist which she turned down.

When she was fifteen she took an overdose of oxazepam. She was admitted to a general hospital and was unconscious for twenty-four hours before being sent home. Subsequently she wrote to the child psychiatrist begging to be found somewhere to live away from home. A social worker from the child guidance clinic came to see her at home with the offer that she could go into an adolescent unit. She went to look round the unit and moved in the next day.

It turned out to be a disturbed children's unit with children aged from three to sixteen years. It was supposed to be a six week assessment unit but most children had been there longer. One boy who was sixteen had been there since he was five when it was a unit for mentally handicapped children. Lynda stayed there for fifteen months. While she was at the unit she had appointments with the psychotherapist for fifteen months.

Lynda left school at sixteen with four O-levels and after a few months got a temporary full-time job as a sales assistant. She moved into a bed-sit and when she was seventeen had her son.

When she was nineteen she went to college to take A-levels in English Literature and Psychology. She applied to universities and was given an unconditional offer by a university in the Midlands. She ended up getting a D grade in English Literature and failing Psychology but moved to the midlands to study for a BSc. Hons. in Education and Psychology. She was on anti-depressants or anxiolytics most of the time that she was at university and had to withdraw from the course after two years because of her health problems. She then worked part-time as a children's nanny for three years and took an Open University course in Personality, Development and Learning.

At the age of thirty she had a complete mental breakdown and was admitted as an emergency to a mental health unit as a voluntary patient. She was there for a month and was prescribed Prozac.

She was referred to a Community Psychiatric Nurse a few months after being discharged from hospital and he arranged for her to be prescribed an anti-psychotic.

After two years of being unable to do anything she did a part-time creative writing course to alleviate the boredom. Over the next few years she went on to do part-time voluntary work with a local MIND association, as a volunteer assistant youth worker with the education service and as a volunteer doing administration for a mental health inpatient advocacy service.   During this time she had art therapy for several years.   She also participated in user-involvement in the planning and development of mental health services for three years.

She gave up doing voluntary work and participating in user-involvement because she grew frustrated with them and because of the difficulty of attending reliably due to her sleep disorder. However, she continued writing. She has written short stories but Dreams of Death is her first novel.

Lynda wrote this novel for several reasons. She is not confident about talking, and writing enabled her to express some things about her own experience of mental illness and the mental health system and the experiences of other people she knew. She wanted to produce something that was more realistic and a counterbalance to the 'psycho on the loose' type of material prevalent in the media and entertainment; and she wanted to write something that would raise awareness and insight into mental illness and the mental health system in an accessible and entertaining way.

In about 2000 her GP stopped her anti-psychotic medication and a year later suffering from delusions she took an overdose of paracetamol that led to her being admitted to a specialist liver unit and then spending two months in a mental health unit.

Lynda has not been in hospital since. Over the years she was in the mental health system she experienced most types of mental health services but has given up on these and continues just on medication from her GP.   She remains unable to work in mainstream employment because of her sleep disorder and mental health problems but she continues to write when she has the motivation and concentration. She has already started writing a childhood memoir and aims to continue writing for as long as possible.

Dreams Of Death

CHAPTER ONE

A seemingly mundane Saturday in February Nineteen eighty – eight, was for differing reasons to be an unforgettable day for Neil Soames, Elizabeth Lingwood, Lyndsay Redmond and Katharine Baines. The air in Bergrove was still and chilled the skin. The pale sun sulked against a blank grey sky and the birds stayed silent in the trees.

For Neil events began to unfold as he worked as a supermarket manager. 'Will Neil Soames come to Customer Service? Telephone call. Neil Soames to Customer Service, telephone call.' The supermarket's public address system made its announcement from an invisible source. The female voice was business-like but had an urgent tone. Neil Soames gave a few more instructions to the pimple faced lads filling shelves in the Bread and Cakes aisle. 'I will be back to crack the whip shortly,' he teased them with a smile before he made his way to Customer Service.

He dodged his way between the bustling customers, and the obstacle course of their shopping trolleys flicking a brief glance down each aisle. Passing he made automatic checks that all was in order, and mentally noted where shelves were looking to be in disarray or sparsely filled. The smells of fresh fish from the counter at one end of the aisle, and washing powder from the other end combined in the middle to create a peculiar hybrid odor. Numerous snatches of everyday life reached him. By the frozen vegetables an elderly woman's mouth contorted around criticism she hissed at her shame faced husband. In the next aisle a little girl in a pushchair called out jubilantly to the world at large.

At the Customer Service desk the matronly assistant smiled and pointed Neil to one of the phones. Mm, she thought as she watched him pick up the phone. He was a bit on the short side, five foot five or six she would guess, but he was a good looking young man. He had endearingly curly but neat brown hair, and merry hazel eyes. She could see why the young

cashiers giggled self-consciously when he was around. If he had been single and she had been a decade or so younger she would have snapped him up herself.

She watched him put the receiver to his ear. 'Hello, Neil Soames speaking' he said authoritatively. She heard his sharp intake of breath and noticed his hands clench round the receiver. 'Yes I will get there as fast as I can' he said into the phone, then turning to her, 'Doreen would you do me a favour? Call the senior manager and tell him I've had to leave. It's an emergency.'

The car park was packed solid with cars of every size, shape and colour. One car was blocking him in. The couple inside were talking animatedly, arms flapping. Even by the time Neil had got in his car, put his seatbelt on, revved the engine and taken the handbrake off the other car was still behind him. Neil punched the horn and twisted round to see what the hold- up was. The driver behind looked his way, raised his hands apologetically and carried on talking to his passenger.

Neil willed himself to cool his frustration. The noise and chaos of the car park receded. The unexpected phone call had left him feeling stunned. He had the sensation of being totally cut off from the world. After blasting the horn urgently twice more, Neil had watched with mounting frustration as the passenger got out and slowly unstrapped a baby from the back seat of the car blocking him. Neil glared at her, but she turned her head away and carried on talking to the driver of the car for a few minutes before sauntering into the shopping centre. The driver pulled away. 'Hallelujah!' Neil said under his breath as he reversed out of his space engine revving and tyres squealing. At the car park exit
he was held up again, this time by the queue of cars waiting to get out across the stream of traffic on the main road.

***

Elizabeth Lingwood sat at her mahogany dining room table; in her plush house in the expensive area of Bergrove. She was waiting for her father. He was usually a punctual man but today he was late. She was wearing a red embroidered smock top, and jeans. Her broad buttocks spread to the edges of the chair. Her hefty bosom nestled on her unused arm as she leaned on the table, and her pudding-basin haircut framed her unmade up face unflatteringly. She however was a woman too confident of the sharpness of her wits, and the eloquence of her tongue, to be bothered about disparaging thoughts others might have about her appearance.

The bookcases lining the wall in front of her held aged volumes, of Shakespeare, Dickens, Chaucer, classic poetry, reference books on the use of English, as well as more contemporary award winning novels and short story collections. A bowl of lavender and geranium potpourri on the sideboard behind her scented the air delicately.

Her attention was focused momentarily on the range of travel brochures lying on the coffee table. She was eager to look through them so she could plan this year's summer holiday, but that would have to wait. First she had to finish marking Class 4 A's essays on 'How to Tie a Shoelace.'

It was one of her staple menu of titles. It could always be counted on to cause a ripple of dissension amongst the girls; that if she was honest she had to admit she rather enjoyed. She must have a slight sadistic streak. For all their murmurs of disbelief and derision they usually surprised themselves when it came to it and even if they didn't, she knew she had set them a hard, and for most of them an uninspiring title and so she was benevolent in her marking.

There had been more than the usual minor ruckus over the title this time, when a father had rung the school to complain that he had not sent his daughter to Grammar School to be set such juvenile and undemanding rubbish. She had not spoken to the father personally as the headmistress had talked to him. However she had herself followed up with a letter to the father. In it she explained that as their English teacher it was her job to stretch the girls' writing abilities, beyond the usual fodder of the like of 'My Summer Holidays'. Further, that writing an account of 'How to Tie a Shoelace' was in fact a very challenging feat of technical writing, and that she had through the years received stunningly entertaining pieces of work on the subject from girls with imagination, a sense of humour, and a reasonable degree of literary competence.
Elizabeth had felt her honour was upheld and there had been no further communication from the father. His daughter had produced an adequate if mediocre essay. As she fiddled with her pen in preparation for more marking Elizabeth wondered again why her father was late.

***

Sixteen year old Lyndsay Redmond was sitting in a bar in Bergrove high street with her boyfriend Mick Hughes. Lyndsay was nervous. All afternoon she had been trying to tell him something important but she couldn't bring herself to say it. They had met up at 1pm and gone to the pictures to watch a Star Trek movie. Well, to half watch it anyway - when Mick began snogging her, his tongue skating over her teeth, darting deep into her throat, one hand round her shoulders, pulling her into him, the other hand trying to massage both her tits at once.

Afterwards they had wandered through the shopping precinct. The shop window reflections showed them as a preposterous couple. Him five foot eleven inches and weighing seventeen stone, with tree-trunk thighs and hairy bear-paw hands. Her five foot two inches, spindly legs in skin tight jeans, an adolescent bosom in a stretch crop top, a stick thin waist and stomach and bottom as flat as a plank of wood, her hair worn up to make her look older and bright make up, only slightly smudged by his lovemaking. Tottering along on her six inch heels Lyndsay was convinced she passed for a sophisticated twenty years old, but to the unforgiving eye she looked like a tarted up twelve years old.

Mick slung his arm round her, his hand coming up under her armpit, fingertips touching the outer slope of her breast. He grinned at the passersby, pausing now and then to kiss her full on the lips, his soft, wet mouth leaving spittle glossing her lipstick. She knew he was proud of her and wanted everyone to notice them together. He sang 'You are the sunshine of my life' and danced her around, laughing as people stared. Lyndsay blushed deep red but she was a bit proud too. Proud of how smart he looked in his navy suit and tie. Proud of his five o'clock shadow, his bulky frame and bulging muscles. No spotty lout for her. She was courting a full grown man. 'How old is he?' the girls at school would ask disbelievingly.

'Thirty' she would say with a nonchalant flick of her hair and they would look at her with a new respect. They had never much considered her before, the council house kid at Grammar School. It was a joke to them. But now she knew they were dying of jealousy. She needed that envy. She needed to be noticed.

Her parents were too busy screaming at each other to pay any attention to her. It seemed to her as though her parents were in between a piece of elastic trying to run away from each other in opposite directions, only they kept pinging back and colliding in the middle. All their energy was taken up with fighting each other.

Most of the time it would be left to Lyndsay to look after her three brothers: five, ten and fourteen years, and they were wild, tearaways. Always up to some sort of trouble: thieving from the shops, bunking off school, tearing up neighbours' gardens for the sheer hell of it, getting into fights. She couldn't manage them. She would tell her Dad and he would roar at them but they knew he didn't mean it. He thought it was a laugh when they got up to no good. Real boys he would say with approval. Her Mum would yell at them but they weren't afraid of that. They would just cheek her back. Sometimes her mum would chase them round the house threatening to tan their backsides with a slipper but they loved it. They thought it was a hoot running all over the furniture, ducking and diving to get out of her way. All this would go on while Lyndsay was trying to do her homework. It often drove her to tears.

But she didn't feel so bad now she had Mick. He appreciated her if nobody else did. He told her she was beautiful. He said every man who looked at her was eating his heart out for her. She was his sweet baby. 'You're like a rosebud about to blossom' he had told her. She thought it was poetic. She felt she existed only when she was with Mick, with him she was someone special. People didn't give her any grief when she was with him. They didn't hassle her, talk down to her, or boss her around. Mick made her feel cared for. But would he still care about her now?

She felt her stomach lurch. Would she still be his sweet baby? She was afraid he would take it badly. She couldn't bear to lose him. He was all she had.

***

Two hundred miles away in the town of Willerdon two small boys ambled along the path huddled together in a whispered conspiracy. Paul was six and Ben was seven. Katharine Baines, Paul's mother and Jackie Morrison, Ben's mother walked a few feet behind the boys chatting to each other. Paul took after his mother with deep brown eyes and black-brown hair, while Ben was a blue-eyed blond in contrast to his mother's auburn hair and grey eyes. The two women were in their early twenties. They had spent the day taking their sons on an outing to the local zoo. They had just had tea at Jackie's flat, and now Jackie was giving her red setter some exercise by walking Katharine and Paul home to their flat on the other side of the council estate.

The estate around them was vast and dreary. It was on the outskirts of Willerdon, at the opposite end of town from the posh areas and a forty minute bus ride into the town centre. Despite its size the estate had no play areas for the children. Only a dilapidated and vandalized shopping centre consisting of a general store, off-license, fish and chip shop and launderette broke up the monotonous uniformity of the houses and flats. As they all approached the block of flats where Katharine and Paul lived the boys turned to their mothers.

'Can Ben come in to play?' Paul asked.

Katharine looked at Jackie.

'Half an hour?' She asked quietly.

'Ok, half an hour only.' Jackie said firmly to the boys. 'It's been a long day and you need a bath and an early night.'

'Oh wicked,' they cheered.

Both mothers knew the truth was that they needed little persuasion to delay the moment when the boys went to bed and they each spent the evening sitting alone in their flats. They were both unmarried mothers. Jackie had become pregnant by a boy in her class at school and Katharine had become pregnant by her ex-social worker within a year of leaving care. Their relationships had broken up as soon as they became pregnant; going against all advice and pressure to have their babies aborted or adopted they had kept them. They perpetually struggled to make ends meet and apart from each other they were virtually friendless, but they took pride in making their sons feel wanted and loved. They had met each other when the boys were both at the same nursery, had realized they lived on the same estate and had become firm friends. Now that Katharine was at college studying A-levels in English Literature and Psychology they didn't see so much of each other during the week but they still met regularly at weekends.

Katharine let them in her flat just as she was gathering letters from the doormat that had come in the late post. Jackie took the dog into the living room while the boys went into Paul's bedroom to play. Katharine gave orange squash to the boys, and then made coffee for herself and Jackie and settled in the living room. One of the letters was obviously a bill so she put it to one side. She opened the other letter, took out a slip of paper and as she read through it her mouth opened in a silent 'Oh' of surprise. Then smiling she waved the slip of paper at Jackie.

CHAPTER TWO

Back in Bergrove it had taken Neil over an hour to reach the hospital amidst the Saturday afternoon traffic. There was no car park near the maternity unit. He'd checked that out a few months previously; and both the car parks adjacent to the General hospital were full and overflowing. In fact there were cars crammed everywhere. There were vehicles on both sides of the road, on the pavements and on the grass verges. He spent ten minutes driving round trying to find a space and eventually had to leave the car in the psychiatric unit car park, and walk back to the maternity unit. As he passed the radiotherapy unit he noticed his hands were stinging and found they were starting to blister where he had been gripping the steering wheel of the car so tight. His mouth was dry, he could smell a faint waft of body odour from his arm-pits, and he was red-faced and breathing hard but at least he was here.

He was led to the labour ward by a young nurse. He had expected to see lots of hi-tech gadgetry but the room was Spartan. Apart from six beds there was nothing else in it. Only two of the beds were occupied. On the far side of the room an older woman in a fleece nightie was propped up on her pillow, rocking from one side of the bed to the other and groaning dramatically. Sarah, Neil's wife was lying still in a bed near the door. She was wearing a hospital gown. Her eyes were closed and her shoulder length layered blonde hair splayed out over the crisp, white pillow, framing her heart shaped face. She was petite, the same height as Neil but in the bed she looked tiny. Her hands, gently cupping her bump, which rose and fell almost imperceptibly with her measured breathing, were delicate. She was twenty-three years old, the same age as Neil but lying there alone, looking fresh-faced and vulnerable Neil thought she could easily pass for a schoolgirl. He stood by the bed and lightly rested his hand on hers.

'Ok love?' He asked softly. She opened her eyes revealing its pale sapphire blue.

'A bit better now' she answered with a faint accent proclaiming her Irish upbringing.

'I was shopping in town with Elizabeth Lingwood; you know my friend from church. I'd been getting twinges all day which were getting worse, so we went for a coffee and a sit down and my waters broke and there was blood in them. The coffee shop staff called the ambulance. Elizabeth followed me to the hospital in her car but she had to leave. She's expecting her dad for dinner and she couldn't get him on the phone to cancel.

'What did the staff say?' Neil asked.

'They've been pretty vague but they seem to think a bit of bleeding isn't that uncommon.' She winced as another contraction started.

'Is it getting worse?' Neil asked.

'No, it's about the same.'

'So, how's Elizabeth?' Neil asked in an effort to distract her from the pain. He was an atheist himself. He believed the bible was myth and legend. No more real than fire-breathing dragons and fairies, but Sarah's faith was important to her and he tried to take an interest.

'She's well. She's planning her summer holiday. We picked up some travel brochures in town. They talked desultorily and then fell into silence. Each time Sarah got a contraction Neil held her hand and rubbed her stomach. Sarah assured him it helped but he wasn't convinced. He felt he was inadequate and redundant. The woman in the other bed had stopped groaning and after being examined by a doctor was up and dressed.

'False labour' she told them cheerily as she packed her bag. 'The four at home are going to be disappointed, they're getting fed up waiting for their new baby brother or sister.' 'We're hopeless novices in comparison then,' Neil said. 'Never mind, we'll soon catch up.' He affected a leer. Sarah arched an eyebrow.

'You want to be careful what you say,' Sarah said with mock menace. 'I might just hold you to it, but you'll have to make Senior Manager before we can add to the tribe we've started here.' She patted her bump. They smiled their goodbyes to the other patient and then they were left alone in the ward as the hours ticked by. Once in a while a nurse would come in and check progress, and after one check the nurse set up a machine by the bed and told them it was a fetal heart monitor. The nurse told them it was routine procedure, but Neil and Sarah looked at each other with new anxiety and the racing beep of the baby's heart set their own hearts palpitating.

The time passed so interminably that it seemed never-ending. Neil's backside was beginning to go numb from immobility. He longed to be able to stretch his legs further than the walk to the toilets. He had been prepared for stress, crisis, and drama. Nobody told you about the boredom. But it was an edgy tedium. The muscles in his back were so tense it felt like they had turned to concrete. Eventually he just had to move.

'I'm going to the car to get a book. Can I get you anything from the hospital shop?' He asked Sarah.

'A magazine. Cosmopolitan? Something light and frothy like that,' she said.

Ten minutes later he was back with a magazine for Sarah and a book on Advanced Management Skills for himself. He settled himself in the chair by the bed and opened the book. He read a few pages but found his thoughts drifting. It was hard to believe that by this time tomorrow he would be a father. This would be the crowning moment of his life so far. He would be a parent, somebody's Daddy. From the time he'd started thinking about which O-levels to take and had begun to question what he really wanted to do with his life, he'd realized that far and above all else he wanted his own family, and just as importantly he wanted his children when he was young enough to enjoy them.

His own parents had been good people, but his mother had been forty-seven when she had him, his father fifty-seven. It was long after they had given up hope of having a child; long after they had lost interest in having a child if the truth were told. Over the years they had developed a cosy, settled routine, just the two of them; and then he had come on the scene disrupting everything. He spoilt their lives and they let him know it. They were always distant and irritated with him. His earliest memory of his mother was of her sinking into a chair, a crocheted shawl wrapped round her shoulders, closing her eyes and tears trickling down her cheeks. He'd gone up to her and rested his hand on her knee and pleaded 'Don't cry Mummy.' She had opened her eyes and looked at him coldly and said, 'Mummy's tired, just play quietly.' Now he could realize she had been exhausted, but at the time it had felt like a shameful rejection.

'Shush, Daddy's tired, just play quietly.' Different versions of that reproach had echoed throughout his childhood. They had never played with him. When he tried to talk to them they always answered in disinterested monosyllables. He so wanted it to be different with his children. He'd chosen his O-levels: English, Maths and Sciences with a view to getting a steady, reliable job so he could support a family. The only frivolity he had allowed himself had been Art. He loved Art. He felt he could communicate through Art on a level playing field. He had been a bit of a misfit at school. The only child who never watched Top of the Pops – his parents disapproved of it and turned it off. Instead they turned the radio on to a classical programme, or put a Gilbert and Sullivan record on their antiquated gramophone player. He was the only boy to have short hair when the trend was for long hair. He was the last boy to go to school in short trousers; and there had always been something a little old fashioned about his demeanour and behavior that set him apart. He had perpetually been just that bit out of synchronization with those around him, too youthful and energetic at home, and with a head too old for his young shoulders at school. It had been a lonely, dreary, vaguely disorientating childhood; for his baby he promised it would be different. He could picture it already. His son or daughter's first smile, first word, first steps. Lavish birthday parties with their friends.

Their first day at school, their first nativity play, brownies or cubs, girl guides or scouts, their first date, their first job. Whatever, whatever they did, whatever they were, he would move heaven and earth to give them the happiest childhood possible.

CHAPTER THREE

At last Elizabeth Lingwood's doorbell rang and she let her father in. This was their ritual ever since she had left University. He would come to her for his Saturday evening dinner and they would talk over the week's events. They both had busy, independent lives. He was retired now but had spent his working life as a general practitioner. Now he occupied his time in other ways. He was Chairman of the Rotary Club and a keen fisherman. Until a couple of years ago he had travelled regularly to the Lake District or to Scotland for the salmon fishing. These days the damp exacerbated his arthritis and he only fished in warm summer weather, but he still followed angling on the television and in specialist magazines. For her own part being Deputy Headmistress kept her occupied. Outside of school hours there were the lessons to prepare, the marking, the paperwork, staff meetings, parents meetings and the supervision of extra-curricular activities. On top of that she had her church interests. She also directed plays with the local amateur theatre group and she went to exhibitions, theatre, cinema and concerts. In the summer holidays she travelled, sometimes alone but often with Joan Hasler the Headmistress who had been her staunch friend ever since she had joined the school, straight out of teacher-training college nearly twenty years ago. It was the same school she had attended as a girl.

On the pale pink walls of her living room, hung picture frames showing montages she had made of postcards and photos from her travels to countries round the world. She had been on painting holidays in France, toured Germany and Italy, cycled through Holland, cruised the Norwegian fjords, back-packed in Australia, tried camel riding in Egypt, gone white-water rafting in Canada, the list could go on. In some of the older photos she was with a boyfriend but there had been no man in her life for a long time now. She suspected she was too self-reliant and strong-minded for most men. She'd had her passions over the years, known a few good, intelligent men whom she had loved and respected. She had relished those relationships – the blissful, the exquisite, the challenging, and she loved a challenge, the arousing, the sweet, all of them had been worth a place in her heart, it was just that none of them were meant to last a lifetime.

And now, well now she was thirty something when the something meant almost forty. She had stopped weighing herself when the scales had shown thirteen stone, and she had gone up at least two dress sizes since then. In addition she found herself sprouting facial hair and burgeoning moles at a disconcerting rate. She had resigned herself without any great regret to spinsterhood and if a man did come along now, well she wasn't quite sure where she would fit him in. She had a well-paid career and plenty of freedom. She was active and fulfilled. Most days she woke up feeling excited, went through the day feeling stimulated, and ended the day feeling rewarded. She was very happy for life to continue exactly as it was. She thought it would be self-indulgent to hanker for more.

'How are you Dad?' She asked and he nodded. 'I tried to ring you this afternoon' she told him.

'I spent the day fishing' he said. She arched an eyebrow.

'In February?'

'I just felt like it' he said irritably. She assumed that he felt he was being lectured on taking more care of his health, so she changed the subject.

'There's a bottle of wine open on the table,' she said as she left him to help himself to a drink while she got the food from the kitchen. 'Could you put some music on Dad?' She called through from the kitchen, and a few minutes later they sat at the table eating roast vegetable quiche, baked potatoes, salad and garlic bread, and drinking white wine to the sound of Tchaikovsky on the stereo. She chatted as they ate. She told him about Sarah Soames going into labour, about the irate parent who had complained about the essay title, about how the teachers were getting nervous because of an upcoming visit from the school inspectors, about the heated debate they'd had at the theatre group on the question of what their next play should be. He nodded and smiled half-heartedly. Eventually she paused. He was always reserved but this evening he seemed unusually uncommunicative.

'You're very quiet Dad?'

'Am I? He said with the same neutral smile. It only strengthened her conviction that he wasn't himself. As a child and a teenager she had thought he was a cold and remote man. It was only as an adult that she had realized it was his shy nature and had begun to feel close to him. Give him procedures and a formal framework to work with and he could handle people well; but she had come to recognize as she grew older that it was only ever his family he felt really at ease with. Since her mum had died she was his only family and lately he didn't even seem at ease with her. It was something she couldn't put her finger on, and it was only tonight that it was gelling into a fully formed awareness in her mind that something was wrong. She experimented in her mind with different ways of phrasing the question but in the end was silent. She was an up-front sort of person herself. She liked things to be straight forward and out in the open, but she didn't want to invade his privacy. She wondered if it was the Rotary Club that was troubling him. The personal politics could get pretty fierce and nasty sometimes, and she knew the responsibility of trying to hold them all together and pulling in the same direction occasionally wearied and worried him, but usually he told her.

He seemed to sense her concern and started talking about this and that – the Rotary Club were planning to build an adventure playground in the summer, for the centre for emotionally and behaviourally disturbed children. They had a new locum working at his old medical practice; his friend Sam had invited him on a joint fishing trip in August, and so on. Elizabeth's anxiety about him began to evaporate. They finished the meal with blueberry muffins and coffee and moved to sit in the living room.

They watched a programme on 'The Life of Birds' together for about an hour and as the credits were rolling Elizabeth asked her father, 'so do you think you will go on the fishing trip with Sam in the summer?' She was puzzled to see him avert his eyes quickly.

'Oh I think I'll wait and see a bit nearer the time,' he said with apparent cheerfulness but his voice was trembling and he kept his eyes downcast. Elizabeth couldn't hold her curiosity back any longer.

'Dad is anything wrong?' He put up his hand to cover his eyes in an attempt to hide his emotion, but then had to bury his face in both hands to conceal the tears trickling down his cheeks. His shuddering shoulders betrayed his silent sobs.

'Dad, what is it?' Elizabeth leaned across and put her hand on his knee. He wrestled a handkerchief from his trouser pocket, and after a few minutes of mopping at his eyes he sat back.

'I've had a bit of news. A bit of bad news,' he managed to say before he started crying again. Elizabeth was impatient to know what would cause her father such distress, but she bit back the urge to press him and let him take his time.

'I wasn't going to tell you' he said, 'not yet, there didn't seem any point worrying you until I know something,' he hesitated, reaching for the right words, 'something more definite.' Elizabeth breathed deeply trying not to let her alarm show or push her into irritation.

'It's well, I have been feeling rather ill for the last few months, and I've had some tests and seen a couple of doctors and they've told me this week that,' he steadied his voice, 'I'm afraid I've got cancer.' Elizabeth was silent, searching for something to say, something that would help, but there was nothing.

'It's not hopeless' he said firmly, 'not yet' he qualified less certainly. Elizabeth guessed he was torn between wanting to relieve her of anxiety, and not wanting to leave her unprepared for the worst.

'Oh Dad, Daddy' Elizabeth said gently, squeezing his hand. She saw the look in his eye, his expression helpless and frightened and she knew what he was thinking.

'It won't be the same Daddy' she urged. 'What happened to Mummy was over twenty years ago. Things have changed, things have got better.'

Elizabeth had been eighteen when her mother had died after a long, traumatic battle against cancer. Elizabeth had sat in her bedroom poring over her A-level revision, while trying to shut out of her mind the sound of her mother crying in the room next door. When she went downstairs to get a drink, she would see her father standing motionless outside her parents' bedroom door. He hovered unable to bring himself to go in and face his wife's suffering, but equally unable to tear himself away and leave her to bear her pain alone and unobserved. It was an image that remained with Elizabeth still.

'Have they, what exactly have they said Daddy?' Elizabeth prompted.

'Well,' he cleared his throat. His voice was gruff, but the persona of the authoritative medical man slid into place. 'It's too soon to be definite about how they are going to approach it, they need to do some exploratory tests, but surgery is a possibility probably backed up by some radiotherapy or chemotherapy.'

Elizabeth nodded. So this was it. He was a doctor. He must have known or at least suspected for some time. All these weeks, how many weeks she wondered, had he been hiding this from her and until today, she hadn't even sensed that anything was wrong. So it wasn't the bloody Rotary Club troubling him after all, not at all.

CHAPTER FOUR

Still in the pub with Mick, Lyndsay swallowed the last of her lager. Mick had to go to work at 9pm so she had to tell him soon. They needed to talk about it. She wouldn't get into the nightclub where he worked. They'd tried it once and the management had words with him. They'd told him they weren't about to lose their license on account of the doorman sneaking his underage bit of totty in, and if he did it again he'd be out of a job. So it had to be now. She'd been putting it off for weeks, and she didn't have much time. The doctor had said she needed to make a decision, whether to have an abortion soon or it would be too late. She looked into Mick's eyes. He had huge round blue eyes, intense blue. She knew she should've taken more care, but the doctor always looked at her so snootily and disapproving when she went for the pill. She hated going. So she'd put it off, taken a chance, trusted to luck. She'd felt like she'd be lucky with Mick, but now? She didn't feel so lucky.

'Mick?' – Her voice was quavering, imploring.

'What is it baby?' He leaned towards her smiling, eyes twinkling.

'I'm…I'm pregnant.' She didn't dare look at him, her lip was trembling. Silence. She sipped at her empty lager glass for something to do, to steady herself. When at last she raised her eyes slowly to look at him he was sitting back, pulling away from her, his eyes narrowed his expression grim. He let out a heavy sigh.

'Lyndsay, why didn't you take care?'

'I'm sorry Mick, I'm sorry,' and she started to weep.

'Don't cry honey, don't cry,' she could tell he was really trying to make it gentle, but there was an edge to his voice. She sniffled and gazed at him helplessly. She could see him getting irritated.

'Christ I thought you had more bloody sense Lyndsay ,' he blurted out.

'I'll get rid of it Mick, it won't be a problem, we can be the same,' she pleaded.

'You haven't told anyone?' He demanded. She hung her head.

'Just my parents.'

'Thank god you're the legal age. You'd end up putting me behind bars. What did your parents say?'

'Dad called me a slag.' Tears welled in her eyes again. 'He called you a few choice names as well. Mum said I should tell you that we should decide what to do together. Dad said I wouldn't see you for dust if I told you, but I thought Mum was right.' Her voice trailed off. She looked at him expectantly. He stared back at her with a hard look in his eyes that she'd never seen before. The silence started to feel menacing.

'What do you want me to do?' She whispered. He stared at her a few moments longer.

'Do what you bloody like,' he snarled and got up and walked off.

***

Lyndsay walked home. She couldn't stop crying, and she didn't want to embarrass herself in front of other passengers on a bus. The darkness hid her tears
from the few other pedestrians. By the time she got half way home her shoes were crippling her, so she took them off and walked barefoot for the last half mile or so. The path felt gritty under her feet. She got home and let herself in. The house was strangely still. Her mother was sitting in an armchair in the living room in front of the gas fire. Her mother's face was puffy and red round the eyes.

'Mum?'

'Well, did you tell him?' Her mother asked sharply. Lyndsay nodded.

'Dad was right. Mick doesn't want to know.' Her mother grunted her dismay.

'It'll have to be an abortion then.' Lyndsay sat down opposite her mother.

'I don't know if I can go through with it.'

'Don't be daft. You don't want to be saddled with a baby on your own at your age.'

'I can't see it as just a ball of cells, you know what I mean? It's a person. It's a live human being I'm carrying. I've lost Mick whatever I do so I might as well have it. At least I'd still have a part of him.

'You're in cloud cuckoo land girl. It's not a person. It's a lump of jelly. It won't be a person for a long time yet and if you kept it where will you live? I don't want a baby under my feet again. I've had four. I've had enough of it and what would you do for money? You'd barely be able to feed yourself on benefits, let alone pay for clothes and bills and stuff for the baby.'

'I'd manage Mum.'

'No you wouldn't, take it from me. What about your education? I've got high hopes for you. You've got a brain. You could make something of yourself my girl. Or do you see yourself sitting your exams eight months pregnant?' Lyndsay couldn't think of an answer. 'You want to get yourself back to the doctors and get an abortion as fast as you can. The sooner the better. It'll only get harder the longer you leave it.'

'Yeah, alright Mum, don't go on about it.'

'Abortion was hardly heard of when I had you. If it had been then...'

'Then you wouldn't have had me. Thanks a lot Mum.'

'What I mean is if I hadn't had you and the boys I could have had a different life.'

'A better life?'

'I wouldn't have stuck with your father all these years for a start.'

'Where is Dad? And the boys? It's dead quiet.'

'They've gone, up and left the lot of them. Your Dad's moved in with his latest bird and the boys have gone with him.'

'That was sudden.'

'No it wasn't. I've known about her nearly two years. Your Dad told me they'd been planning this at least six months. She got some money from her divorce and she's taken on a mortgage and bought them a house.'

'It won't last Mum, none of his other women ever do.'

'This one's different. He'd have run a mile if any of the others had asked him to move in.'

'So where've they gone?'

'Wouldn't tell me. Said he didn't trust me not to go and smash the windows in.'

'But how are you going to see the boys?'

'I'm not, unless they come home. Good riddance anyway. They had me tearing my hair out. If they prefer to be with their Dad it's their lookout. It's only because he lets them get away with murder they chose to be with him. I might miss Will, he's my baby,' she conceded, 'but he gets more like his loutish brothers and his bone idle father every day.'

So this was why her Mum's eyes were red Lyndsay thought, but it'd be no use trying to console her she'd just get more pigheaded that she didn't care.

'I wish I could do something for you Mum,' was all she could think of to say.

'Don't worry about me girl I'm a tough old boot, I can look after myself. The best thing you can do for me is to get your own little problem sorted out. Then I'll have one thing less to worry about.'

***

Inside Mr.J's nightclub, mirror balls sparkled and reflected the flashing disco lights in sexy pink flushes, or alien hues of blue and green on the gleaming faces, and thrashing bare limbs of the young people convulsing on the dance floor.

Mick Hughes had just started work and was prowling up and down by the doorway. People were thronging to get in but he let his colleague Terry check them in. Mick didn't trust himself to speak civilly to anyone. He was still fuming over Lyndsay. He'd wanted the pliable temperament and lithe body of a girl, with the mind of a woman. Now he was faced with the mentality of a schoolgirl, and the soon to be matronly body of a pregnant woman. Christ he really didn't need this. The more he thought about it the more angry he got. If his mates heard about this he'd be a laughing stock. He'd preened over Lyndsay in front of them. The women he knew would probably spit in his eye for getting a schoolgirl pregnant. He prided himself on having a way with the ladies without ever getting tied down, but also without making himself look like a total bastard. One way or another though, when this got out it was going to sour his image.

In a lull in the queue to get in, Terry watched him scornfully.

'What the fuck's the matter with you Mick? You're pacing like a bitch on heat.' He shouted over the music which was blaring so loud they could feel the vibrations passing through their bodies. Mick heaved a sigh. He couldn't keep this to himself. It was winding him up.

'Look don't tell anyone right?' He waited for Terry to nod his assent. He moved closer to Terry so he could speak in his ear. 'It's Lyndsay, she's pregnant.'

'Silly little bitch! Didn't I tell you? I told you she'd be trouble.'

'Yeah well it's done now.'

'Is it yours?'

'Of course it's sodding mine.' But to be honest Mick hadn't thought to question it. Now that he did his doubts evaporated in seconds. Lyndsay adored him. He knew he could trust her.

'You told her to get rid of it pronto, I hope?'

'Mm, sort of.'

'What d'you mean sort of? You're a bloody fool. The little cunt'll take you for every penny you make in maintenance if you let her have it.

'Don't talk about her that way Tez, she's a good kid.'

'Do you want to be tied to a nagging girl and a squalling baby? Christ you're soft. Twist her arm. Put the fear of god into her. Tell her she gets rid or her face won't look so pretty.' Mick looked at Terry uneasily. They were old mates but right now he wanted to get away from him.

'Look I'm going to sneak a quick break, see if I can get my head together. Look after the door?' Terry agreed and Mick went to the bar for a coke. He sat thinking over what Terry had said. He was still angry but the object of his anger had changed from Lyndsay to Terry. Lyndsay might have messed up, but he wouldn't hurt her in a million years and he didn't like the way Terry talked about her. Terry's bigotry had made him question himself. Maybe he wasn't being fair to Lyndsay. She was just a kid and he hadn't taken precautions either. Would it be so bad to be hitched up to her on a permanent basis? It was the first time the thought had occurred to him. She was a cute looker and she worshipped the ground he walked on. He could do a lot worse and he had to face it, his time as Jack the Lad was fading. He was overweight with a rapidly swelling beer gut. Women his own age didn't give him a second glance anymore. To stay in the game he had to rely on his ability to impress ever younger girls. The way he was going, ten years from now he'd just be another middle-aged lech hanging round school gates. It wasn't a prospect that appealed to him. He wasn't taken with the idea of being Dad to a screaming baby either, he couldn't pretend otherwise but babies grew up. It could be a son. He wouldn't mind taking a lad to footie matches. Actually he'd be proud, he suddenly realized. It'd show the world he had real lead in his pencil. He took another sip of his coke. He couldn't believe he was really thinking like this. He shook his head – bemused by himself. He felt really confused. He wished he could talk it over with someone other than Terry. Someone who wouldn't just tell him to get effing serious.

Dreams Of Death

CHAPTER FIVE

In Willerdon Katharine Baines was still smiling. Jackie and Ben were leaving.

'A big congratulations again' Jackie said, giving Katharine a big hug.

'I still can't believe they've given me an unconditional offer. I've got a place at University Jackie,' she laughed. 'The pressure is off. It doesn't matter what grades I get in my A-levels, I've got a place anyway. The interview must have gone better than I thought. In October I'm going to be starting at Bergrove University! If this goes to plan three years from now, I'll be a graduate. This could lead to a much better life for Paul and me.

Dreams Of Death

Lynda Anning

CHAPTER SIX

On the maternity ward Neil was listening carefully to the fetal heart monitor.

'Sarah, am I imagining it or is the beeping getting slower?' Sarah opened her eyes and listened.

'I'm not sure.' Both of them listened intently. 'You're right,' she said with alarm, 'it's slowing down, buzz the nurse Neil.' Neil pressed the buzzer. They waited but nobody came.

'I'm going to look for someone,' he said 'just try to keep breathing evenly.' There was no-one in sight as he hurried down the corridor. He knocked on an office door but was answered with silence. He was feeling panicky. He half-turned on his heels but he didn't know the layout of the hospital, he didn't know where else to look. He tried rapping on the office door again louder. Christ somebody had to be on duty. There was a muffled sound from inside. He opened the door to see a bleary-eyed, white-coated doctor rising slowly from his chair.

'Yes' the doctor said warily, seeing Neil's mixed expression of anger and desperation.

'It's the baby. The heart beats slowing.'

'Right, I'm on my way. Sorry I was a bit slow to answer the door, thirty-six hour shift,' the doctor smiled ruefully.

Once the doctor had examined Sarah it seemed to Neil like pandemonium broke out. The doctor told him that he had done the right thing fetching him. The baby was showing signs of distress. They had to get it out as fast as possible. They would try a forceps delivery but if that didn't work, it would have to be an emergency caesarian.

Sarah was rushed to the delivery room with Neil at her side. She was fearful and crying. She gripped Neil's hand. The doctor told her to push. Sarah cried out in between taking big gasps of pain-relieving gas from the face mask. Neil could see the crown of the baby's head. The next minute the doctor commanded Sarah to stop pushing, saying the umbilical cord was caught round the baby's neck. The doctor carefully eased the cord free and coaxed Sarah to push again with the next contraction. Suddenly it was all over. Neil had been warned by other parents to expect a wailing, wrinkled, prune-skinned newborn infant, but this tiny creature was beautiful, smooth-skinned, legs tucked up under her body, her knees against her stomach, her miniature hands curled under her chin.

She didn't cry but seemed to be asleep, a look of blissful tranquility on her face. The realization that she wasn't crying, wasn't moving jolted Neil. 'Is she all right?' He asked. The nurse didn't answer but cut the cord and whisked the baby away to be weighed and checked.

To Neil it seemed like an eternity before they brought her back, wrapped in a blanket and laid her in Sarah's arms.

'Put her to the breast,' the nurse told Sarah, 'she's fine. Congratulations you have a beautiful baby girl.' Neil leant his head against Sarah's forehead as they both wept tears of relief.

'Do you want to hold her?' Sarah asked him after the baby had suckled for a few minutes. Cagily he put one hand under the tiny bundle, the other hand supporting her head and held her close to his chest. He felt the most ecstatic, thrilling feeling sweep over him. This was the most extraordinary, magical moment of his life. As he held her the baby opened her eyes. Her gaze wandered until she was looking directly at him with a bright, alert look.

'She's looking at me,' he said softly to Sarah.

'A newborn's vision is unfocused, she can't see anything clearly,' the nurse scoffed. But Neil didn't believe her. He was sure he had seen awareness in the baby's eyes. She seemed to scrutinize him with a slight frown that looked so adult, and self-possessed that it made him laugh.

All the tension of the past hours slipped away and he felt invigorated. He gave the baby back to Sarah to hold, and laid his hand on Sarah's arm.

'How are you feeling? He asked her.

'Very sore and very exhausted, I'm not doing this again in a hurry.' Neil put his arm round Sarah and stroked the baby's hair.

'Welcome to the world Anna,' he said softly and kissed the baby's head.

'Welcome Anna,' Sarah echoed and kissed the baby too.

'And thank you Sarah,' Neil said, kissing his wife. 'You've made me the happiest man in the world. I feel fantastic.'

CHAPTER SEVEN

It was a Saturday three months later. Neil was at work and Elizabeth was visiting Sarah and the baby. They sat in Sarah's living room drinking coffee and chatting, while Anna laid kicking her legs and gurgling contentedly in her bouncy chair. Elizabeth had been to the house many times before so the lilac painted walls, the grey carpet, the three piece suite and the photos on the mantelpiece of Sarah's parents in Ireland, of Neil's late parents and of Neil and Sarah on their wedding day were not new to her. Only the photos of Anna, the heart-tugging talc and lotion smell of baby, and the glint of pride in Sarah's eyes were recent changes.

Elizabeth was feeling rather down, but didn't want to burden Sarah with her troubles. She hid her depression behind a cheerful interest in the baby, which Sarah responding to happily.

'We haven't quite got her sleeping through the night yet,' Sarah told Elizabeth. 'So both Neil and I are rather tired but on the whole she's very good. She's had a bit of a cold the past few days but she's not fretful. We got our first photo of her smiling last week, look.' The picture showed Neil cradling Anna in his arms. She had her mother's big violet blue eyes, a few wisps of fine blonde hair and a wide gummy smile that matched her Daddy's grin.

'It looks as though Neil is good with her,' Elizabeth said.

'He's great. I get up with her when he's working because she naps during the day and I can catch up on some sleep, but Neil gets up for her in the night when the next day is his day off and he can have a lie-in. He changes nappies, gives her a bottle sometimes just so he can experience feeding her, and when he's home on time he gives her a bedtime bath. He simply dotes on her. She absolutely loves him to bits. He's brilliant with her. He makes my job a lot easier. He's babysitting her tonight so I can go out. I haven't been out on my own since she was born so it will be a nice break.'

'Are you going anywhere special?'

'I'm going out with some of the other women from the solicitor's office, where I worked before having the baby. Hey I've been talking about myself and the baby the whole time you've been here. How are you? How is your Dad getting on?'

'Well,' Elizabeth unconsciously ran her finger round the rim of her coffee cup, 'to be honest things are not too good. I've just come from Dad's. He is reacting badly to the treatment they are giving him. It is making him very sick and ill, and he is such a pig-headed so and so. Well, no, it is not pig-headedness it is shyness really but he won't have anybody go in to look after him. He is not so ill he needs to be in a hospital, and he would much rather not be in hospital but he really should not be on his own. So … I have cancelled my holiday, and I have made a decision to leave work and have Dad move in with me so I can look after him.'

'That's a sacrifice.'

'I know he would rather stay in his own house but I don't want to be away from my home as well as my work. For my own peace of mind I need to know he is being looked after, and he won't let anyone else do it.'

'Has he agreed to this?'

'Yes, grudgingly, but he has agreed. I'm going to get a room ready for him this week and he is going to move in next weekend. I've given my notice at work and I'll leave at the end of term. If and when he is well again he can go back home but this might be the last time I have with him. I want to make it the very best I can for him. It is going to completely transform my life though.' She didn't say how miserable that made her feel.

***

Mick Hughes paced up and down the steps of the red brick building.

'Do I look all right?' He asked Terry.

'You look pretty as a picture' Terry replied sarcastically. 'Look Mick, you don't have to go through with this. There's still time for you to change your mind.' Mick fiddled with the white carnation in his button-hole.

'Jeez Terry, you're supposed to be my best man. When are you going to get it through your thick head? This is what I want. I've thought about it till my head's spinning. I want to marry Lyndsay, and even if I didn't there's no way I would leave the poor kid on the steps of the registry office.

Meanwhile Lyndsay and her Mum were talking in the taxi bringing them to the registry office.

'We're going to be late Mum!'

'We're not going to be late. The taxi'll only take a few more minutes to get there.'

'I'm going to miss you Mum.'

'You'll be alright. You've got Mick to look after you now.' Privately Betty had doubts about how much use Mick Hughes would be at looking after Lyndsay, but there wasn't really a better option as Lyndsay wouldn't have an abortion. That's what Betty had decided when Lyndsay had asked her permission to marry, and there was no point saying anything now that would spoil her daughter's day.

'Anyway you can always come and see me. I won't be far away.'

'It's going to be a struggle to get across town with a buggy though. I'll have to get two buses.

'I'm not going to be across town much longer. As soon as you're settled in with Mick I'm putting the house on the market. I'm going to sell it and buy something bigger on the cheap side of the city.'

'Mum that's daft. There's only you to live in it.'

'I'm going to live on the ground floor and have the rest converted into bedsits so I can make some money. I can't work with my thyroid trouble and high blood pressure, and I can't manage on the benefit I'm getting since your Dad left.'

'Make him pay you some maintenance Mum.'

'I don't know where he is, and I don't know if he's working. It's not worth the aggravation. I'd rather be independent of him anyway.'

'What about the boys? They won't know where to find you.'

'They've made their choice. I'm not spending the rest of my life sitting on my bum waiting for them to decide to pay me a visit.'

They had to stop talking as the taxi drew up outside the registry office. Lyndsay got out and went to Mick.

'Do I look ok, lover?' She asked him quietly. He looked at her gazing at him, wide-eyed in her pink and white maternity dress and white sandals.

'For six months pregnant you look fantastic.' He could see she was hurt by the look in her eyes. He realized he'd been clumsy to qualify his praise. 'You look fucking fantastic' he reassured her and squeezed her hand. She beamed a smile. The little gathering complete, they went into the registry office to take their wedding vows. Betty hid her cynicism and even Terry put on a cheerful face for the proceedings, but inwardly they each had little hope that the marriage would last much beyond the honeymoon.

***

Katharine Baines was visiting her friend Jackie with her son Paul. The boys were playing army in Ben's bedroom and the two women were chatting in the living room. Katharine looked round the familiar room. It felt cosy and welcoming. Why it was that she always felt so much more at home in Jackie's flat, than she did in her own was a thought she wondered at. Perhaps it had something to do with growing up in care. She was desperately tired. She slouched in the arm chair, feeling as though she would never have the energy to move again. Even talking felt like an effort.

'How's the revision for you're A-levels going?' Jackie asked. Katharine rolled her eyes.

'Not very well. I'm revising day and night but I just don't seem to remember it, and it's hard to concentrate. It makes it very difficult to study. I open a book or look at my notes and my mind just floats away. I sit in a sort of trance for hours. I'm worried about Paul. I've lost track of how many times his teacher has called me into school to complain about his behavior in class over the last term. I feel like it's my fault but I don't know what I should do about it. He's really good at home, but I'm permanently exhausted. I'm really worried I'm going to fail my exams.'

'At least you know you've got your place at University no matter what happens,' Jackie said so as to console her.

'I know, at least there is that, but it doesn't bode well. If this is what I'm like taking A-levels, how on earth am I going to manage a degree?

CHAPTER EIGHT

When Neil got home from work that evening he and Sarah had their tea. Afterward Neil washed up while Sarah fed Anna, bathed her, dressed her in a yellow baby grow and put her to bed in her cot. Sarah showered, fixed her hair and make-up and changed into fresh clothes. Neil made himself a mug of coffee and went and sat in the wicker chair beside Anna's cot, and started reading to her from a Ladybird book. He knew it was silly. She wasn't going to understand it at three months old, but he loved the feeling of sitting with her and reading to her as she babbled appreciatively.

The elation he had had at her birth had stayed with him for days. She had had a little jaundice at first but it had been easily treated and after six days they had taken her home. As the weeks and months passed she was the picture of thriving good health. She gained a good amount of weight and was responsive to everyone. Despite her runny nose over the past few days she was still feeding well and seemed unbothered by her sniffles. Neil stopped reading for a moment to watch her. Her fractional movements and the shifting expressions on her face never failed to fascinate him. Sarah put her head round the door.

'I'm off.'

'Have a lovely evening,' Neil told her, 'don't hurry back. I've got everything under control.'

'Ok, but remember you said that when I roll in drunk at five in the morning having partied wildly all night,' she teased.

Neil continued reading to Anna until she fell asleep, and then he picked up his sketch pad and pencil and drew a picture of her slumbering. When he was satisfied with his effort he switched the baby monitor on and settled himself downstairs in the living room.

He read the paper and a couple of chapters from his book on advanced management skills, did the crossword and then watched a comedy on the television.

At ten o'clock he prepared Anna's bottle. He took it up to her and stood for a few moments gazing at her hesitantly. She was lying on her stomach with her face to the wall. It seemed a shame to wake her. He debated with himself whether to leave her sleeping and warm her bottle up later when she woke up. As he was trying to decide he became aware of a twinge of anxiety. He couldn't quite put his finger on what it was but..., and then it leaped into consciousness. She was lying so perfectly still, as still as a statue, too still.

He put the bottle down and pulled the quilt back quickly and picked her up. As he touched her, a jolt of terror went through him. She was limp and cold. He turned her towards him, and with horror saw that her face and lips were a bluish grey. As he ran downstairs to the phone he clutched her to him, hugging her close, trying to give her his body heat as though it could warm her back to life. Neil rang the number for emergency services. The voice that answered was female with a hint of a Bergrove accent. Neil tried to keep his thoughts straight and speak clearly but it was hard, the operator seemed so slow and pedantic.

'What service? Name? Address? What's the problem?

'I think my baby's dead' he screamed down the receiver. The voice at the other end was silent for a few moments and then a new voice came on.

'The ambulance is on its way.' The voice continued calmly, deliberately asking for more details. How old was the baby? Was the baby stiff or floppy? Was there anything unusual about the baby's colour? Was the baby breathing? Could he feel a heartbeat? Then the voice continued carefully, slowly, to give him instructions for artificial resuscitation.

'Cradle the baby along one arm with your hand supporting its head. Check that the baby hasn't swallowed its tongue and that its airway is clear.' There was a pause. 'Is the airway clear?'

'Yes,' Neil answered hoarsely. He tried to let the voice reassure him, and give him confidence that he could do this right and it could work. The voice went on, evenly measured.

'Hold the baby with its head tilted back. Cover the baby's nose and mouth with your mouth and puff in gently making its chest rise. Then remove your mouth and watch the chest fall. Neil did as he was told. 'Do the same again, then using two fingers press down no more than an inch in the middle of the baby's breastbone. Press down once a second fifteen times. Now breathe into the nose and mouth again twice.' At this point the doorbell rang. Neil shot up to answer the door.

'Help her,' he begged bundling Anna into the ambulance man's arms. The man laid Anna on the settee and examined her. He turned to Neil awkwardly.

'I'm sorry' he said, 'there's nothing we can do. She has been gone quite some time.'

'There must be something you can do' Neil pleaded. 'She was alive at six o'clock, gone six.'

'I'm really sorry, she's dead, she's been dead a good couple of hours I would say, much too long to resuscitate. There is nothing we can do for her now,' the man said gently. Neil collapsed onto the settee and picked Anna up and held her tight in his arms. 'I have to ring your doctor and get them to certify the death, and I have to ring the police,' the man said. 'It is routine procedure to report a sudden unexplained death.' Neil leaned back feeling faint. Oh dear god if he could only will her little chest to rise, her heart to beat, for her to splutter and come back to life. He would give anything to be able to return this moment to normality. He squeezed his eyes tight shut, and pressed his lips together to suppress the groan forming in his throat. But the worst wasn't over yet. How in the name of Jesus was he going to tell Sarah?

***

In the pub with her friends Sarah was laughing. She was a bit merry and having a good time. This group of friends got on well together, and they had been chatting animatedly all evening about work, boyfriends, husbands, films, television, holidays and of course the baby. Sarah was the first of the group to have a baby
and it was making them all feel broody. They discussed Sarah's return to work. Originally she had planned to return to work when her maternity leave finished, but as she told her friends now Anna was actually here she felt differently. She wanted to be with the baby, to see her grow up. Now she was thinking she would wait till Anna started school before she went back to work. Her friends nodded sympathetically and the conversation moved on.

It was eleven thirty pm when Sarah got home. Her giggly mood vanished abruptly when she opened the door to see the family doctor, and a policeman in the living room. They had persuaded Neil to put Anna back in her cot, so Neil's strained and ashen face made Sarah's first thought be that he was ill. The three men shuffled uncomfortably looking at one another and then at Sarah, but it was Neil who told her that Anna was dead. She heard him forcing the words out, saw he was wrestling to control his emotions, hardly able to look her in the face apart from a flicker of surprise the news hardly seemed to register with Sarah. She scanned the faces of the doctor, the policeman and Neil as if trying to discern what might lie behind the playing of such a cruel joke. Then she turned suddenly and wordlessly ran upstairs to Anna's room.

Neil followed her upstairs. She stared wildly round the room as though seeing it for the first time. Her gaze tracked from the clown alphabet frieze on the wall, to the dancing bears musical mobile that played Whistle a Happy Tune, to the cot with the quilt covered in cartoon characters. She pulled the quilt back gingerly and picked Anna up. She hugged her, her head bent low over the little body, kissing her and murmuring to her. She looked up at Neil with a look of beseeching helplessness. Then she started to scream.

CHAPTER NINE

Two years later Sarah Soames and Elizabeth Lingwood, still firm friends, were sitting together in Elizabeth's sitting room. Elizabeth was feeling restless. The house was as always clean and tidy. She had the same comfortable furnishings she'd had for years. She had a lavender perfumed candle lit on the mantelpiece, and the atmosphere was cosy, but the comfort and cosiness jarred on her nerves. Day in and day out she had no release from these surroundings. Each morning she saw the same colours and felt the same textures. She knew every whir, click and hum of the house the way a musician knows every note and half beat of an often played piece of music. The constancy of it all smothered her.

These days it was only Sarah and the headmistress from school who came to visit her, and when they had gone she would sit in the high-backed chair by the bay window looking out at the world. She sat there every day after she had finished the housework, and gave in to one kind of boredom only to find another kind in the passionless dross of daytime television. For short bursts of time though she enjoyed watching at the window. She would see tree branches dipping and rising in the breeze, birds flying of just pecking at the ground, occasionally people walking along the road. Her pleasure was blemished however by the pang of envy that tugged at her stomach, and brought sudden tears streaming to her eyes. The days when she had walked down that road seemed a distant, half-remembered dream.

The problem had started during her father's illness. Caring for him had drained her. As he had become increasingly more ill, she had spent more and more time nursing him. She had not only given up work. One by one she had stopped directing the theatre group, stopped going to church, stopped doing anything except shopping, washing, dressing and feeding her father, taking him to hospital appointments and trying to be a devoted companion to him through his final months. In a strange way it had been anti-climax when he died.

She had arranged and attended his funeral, but that was one of the last few times she had left the house. She couldn't remember now when she had first realized that she had a problem. She knew it was long after she had first felt a stomach churning when she was out, after the first time the noise in the coffee shop had dinned in her ears, and the dizzy feeling had overwhelmed her in the supermarket, that the hot flush had brought the sweat out on her forehead as she walked along the street. Where had she been when she had first felt that urge to scream out loud? When she'd felt the tightness in her chest? The palpitations so hard she'd thought she must be on the verge of a heart attack.

It had seemed natural at first to cut things short. She didn't need to shop so often anyway when it was just for herself. She didn't need to go to the hospital for her father's appointments anymore. She'd lost her faith as she'd watched her father dying, so church was no longer on the agenda. She was still grieving for her father, so her friends understood that she didn't feel like meeting for coffee. Initially they had pressed her for meetings, had still come to the house to visit her but her depression made her so terse and remote with them, that they had tired of the awkward one sided conversations and stopped visiting her. She had started paying a domestic helper to do her shopping and post her letters, and had put her plans to go back to work on permanent hold.

Two weeks ago, Sarah the only friend left who still saw her had talked her into going to see her family doctor. Sarah had practically had to force - march her to get her there but she had succeeded. The doctor couldn't find anything physically wrong with her, but suggested she might be suffering from agoraphobia. He prescribed some tablets for the anxiety and referred her to a Community Psychiatric Nurse.

Today had been the first time the Community Nurse had visited Elizabeth and she was telling Sarah how it had gone.

'He was a lovely chap, but young, only in his mid-twenties. He was very patient and understanding. He explained that in certain situations when I go out I'm experiencing a physical reaction. Too much adrenalin is circulating in my body which is what makes me feel so ill. He plans to see me once a fortnight for about six months, and he is going to teach me some relaxation exercises. He says that once I understand what makes me feel so bad, I can use the exercises to calm the feelings and with time I will find it easier to go out.

'Do you think it is going to be helpful?' Sarah asked.

'I do. I am feeling much more positive. If it just enables me to go back to work, it will be great. I miss teaching so much, but enough about my problems. How are you and Neil?' Sarah sighed and took a deep breath.

'I've made a big decision. I've decided I'm going to leave him. I'm going back to Ireland. I'll stay with my parents until I can sort out my own place.'

'You can't mean it Sarah. You and Neil adore each other. Why? Why would you want to leave him?'

'It is Anna's death. I know I should be getting over it by now… but how I feel about it just won't go away. I blame Neil, I

42

mean, I don't really blame him but I say things to him, cruel things that make him feel I hold him responsible for her death. I wish I didn't but it just comes out. It's guilt really. I blame myself but I can't bear to admit it to him and it comes out as an attack on him. I ask myself if I had stayed at home that night would she still be alive? It has been two years and I still crave the feel, the smell, the sound of her. I got rid of everything after she died you know. After the funeral I made Neil take every last thing of the baby's away. He begged me to let us keep some of her things but I insisted. I don't know why really. I just couldn't bear the sight of them. Now I ransack the house over and over trying to find some small thing of hers to hold, but there is nothing. It's all gone.'

Sarah cupped her face in her hands.

'I still mentally check and re-check everything I did for her the day she died, searching for anything that was different from the usual. I question Neil repeatedly about how he looked after her when I was out. It's obsessive. I know it makes him feel it was his fault but I can't help myself. I can't live with the memories anymore and Neil is a constant reminder. Our doctor told us to try for another baby straight
away after Anna's death, but we were both appalled by that. The last year though Neil has warmed to the idea of having another one but I don't want one. We argue about it all the time now, but I just couldn't trust myself with a child's life ever again. If I leave him, at least he will have the chance to start a family again with someone else.'

'You just need more time.'

Sarah made a wry face.

'It's not a matter of time. I won't have any more children. I've lost two already. I don't want to risk going through it again, it would finish me off.

'Two?'

'I had an abortion when I was seventeen. Neil doesn't know,' she added hastily. 'There was a boy in Ireland. He lived down the road and we were friends and well, things just happened. Then he joined the Royal Marines and was sent to Devon for training. It was supposed to be a big secret, but a jealous ex-girlfriend spread it about and it meant he couldn't come back to Ireland. For an Irish boy to be in the British Armed Forces he'd be considered a traitor back home, it wouldn't be safe for him. When I realized I was pregnant I couldn't tell my parents. My father is a staunch catholic, he would have been mortified, and my mother would just have followed my father's lead. So, I got some money together and came to England to see the boy so we could sort out what to do. Only when I got to his base, I found he had a new girlfriend. In the end I never even told him I was pregnant.'

Sarah ran her finger through her hair distractedly.

'I didn't know what to do. I was in a bit of a state. I stayed in England and had an abortion. Afterwards somehow I couldn't face going back to Ireland. I think I thought if I saw my parents face to face the grief would spill out, and I would tell them about the abortion. They would have been even more horrified than if I had told them I was pregnant in the first place. So I remained in England, got myself on a training course to be a legal secretary and drifted through life for a couple of years. I tried to get to know people, but I couldn't hide my depression and most people kept their distance. Then I met Neil. I think to start with, it was our mutual solitude that drew us together. I told Neil about my boyfriend but I've never told him about the abortion.'

'Some happiness at last' Elizabeth said gently.

'Yes it was. Neil was somber at first. His parents had both died the previous year. His mother had an aneurism and nine months later his father had a heart attack. I hadn't known Neil very long, when I realized for the first time in two or three years I was remembering what it was like to be happy. Neil was kind, he was funny and he was ambitious. Not in a wanting it all way, but motivated. He knew what he yearned for, he knew what he had to do to get it and he was dedicated. He wasn't pretentious or bigheaded. It was exciting listening to him talk about his plans. He exuded a determined, enthusiastic strength. They were such good optimistic times. Neil had just finished the first stage of his management training course. I was
working in my job as a legal secretary, and every moment we weren't working we spent together.'

Elizabeth smiled.

'From a very early stage we were easy and relaxed together. I used to go and watch him playing in the Sunday football league in winter, and cricket in the summer until he damaged his knee and had to give it up. Afterwards we used to go to a place where they did strawberry ice-cream sundaes. Neil was different to other young men his age. He was so committed to having a family. I knew he would make a good husband. You know he gave up the chance of a place at Art College and instead took a place as a trainee manager, because he thought it offered better financial security to raise a family on. I think we both thought we had been through the worst that life could throw at us. That together we could overcome unhappiness and build a rich contented life for ourselves. I can't deprive him of a chance to have his own children. It would eat away at him. I know it all sounds a bit muddled, but I'm sure that what I'm doing is the right thing. Will you do something for me though? He is going to take it very badly. Will you stay in touch with him when I've gone?'   'Of course I'll check he's alright, but I think you're making a mistake. You must talk to him about how you're feeling.'

'I can't. I feel as though Anna died to pay for the life of the baby I aborted. I know I'm not being rational but the guilt plagues me. Neil wouldn't be understanding. He used to go on Pro Life marches when I first knew him. He's a fervent anti – abortionist. I couldn't tell him. I've been thinking about this a long time. I'm determined to leave. I'm going to tell him tonight.'

***

As Elizabeth and Sarah were talking, Lyndsay Hughes was visiting her mother. Still only eighteen years old Lyndsay was - against her mother's expectations - still married to Mick Hughes and now had two sons: Rory born three months after she married Mick, and Jake born a year later. The boys were Mick's image, and she knew Mick was pleased as punch with the little lads but she found it hard managing on her own. Mick was serving a prison sentence for burglary. As a first offence he might have got off with a non-custodial sentence, but there was violence involved. It wasn't Mick who carried out the violence, but he had refused to give the police the name of his accomplice who had attacked the householder. It had gone against him in court and he was serving a twelve month sentence.

The two boys played with lego in Betty's sitting room as their mother and grandmother talked.

'He's served half his sentence with good behavior, he'll probably be home soon,' Betty said, trying to buck her daughter's spirits up.

'I know,' Lyndsay said forlornly, 'but I miss him, the boys miss him. Rory's starting to ask questions. I can't bring myself to tell him his Dad is in you know
where. I tell him his Dad will be coming home but he wants to know when. It's hard to explain time to a kiddy. He wants to know if Daddy is coming home today or tomorrow. He doesn't understand months. All I can say to him is not today and not tomorrow but Dad will come home. The hardest thing is knowing he only did it for me and Rory. He wanted to give us the best of everything. I don't want or need the best of everything. What I want and need is Mick at home with me and Rory and Jake. I think deep down he's really insecure. He can't believe that him and an ordinary wage are good enough for us.

'I always knew he would be trouble,' her mother said sourly.

'Well you didn't do such a great job when you picked my Dad! Have you still not heard anything from him?'

'No. Not a word since the day he walked out.'

'You must miss the boys.'

'If my own sons can't be bothered to get in touch with me, then I'm not going to worry my head about them.'

'Of course it would help if they knew where you lived. I don't reckon you should've ever given up the house. This place is falling to bits. You don't make any money out of it and the tenants are more trouble than they're worth.'

'I get by. I've got my rooms on the ground floor that do me quite nicely thank you, and I make twenty pounds a week out of each of the bedsits upstairs. I wouldn't get that on benefits. Ok I've had a few bad tenants and the place is big and expensive to look after, so it looks a bit shoddy in places, but it's not a bloody hotel I'm running here. It'll do for the likes of what lives in it. You don't want to worry about me my girl, you want to concentrate on keeping your Mick on the straight and narrow.

***

Katharine Baines had passed one A-level and failed the other but with an unconditional offer, she had been able to take up her place at Bergrove University anyway. Two years on she was still at university – just. She had scraped through her first year exams and was now coming up to her second year exams. Little had changed since she had sat her A-levels. She had moved, of course, a couple of hundred miles to Bergrove. She lived with her son in a flat about five miles from the university, and cycled into the university every day. Her son was at the local school but hadn't settled in, and Katharine was getting worn down by the teachers' complaints about his behavior. To help make her grant stretch Katharine worked part-time as a cleaner at the university. It was the only work that fitted around school hours, but it was physically tiring cleaning student accommodation. She ached so much she could hardly sit up straight. She felt at times as though she could barely drag one foot in front of the other. It felt so difficult to move she had begun to fear she had multiple sclerosis, or leukaemia or cancer of the spine.

She went to the doctor's practically every month, but they just kept saying they thought it was depression. The anti-depressants they gave her made no difference, and the doctors' cynical and suspicious looks made her fear they thought she was a hypochondriac, or mad so she stopped going. She teetered along always feeling a bit out of control, never really coping. She had no idea what to do about the school's complaints about her son, struggled painfully to manage her studies and worried day and night about how she was going to pay the bills. She spent hours just sitting in a daze, daydreaming about a better, easier more relaxed way of life, but if that was ever going to be a reality she had to get her degree.

***

46

Neil knelt by Anna's grave in the cemetery and arranged a posy of chrysanthemums in a vase at the head of her pitifully small burial plot. The pain of the first few days after Anna's death, when he and Sarah had sat shivering from the shock, crying continually and drinking countless cups of coffee was now fading. The cold formality of the inquest that had confirmed she died from cot death was long since over. The funeral, the prayers, the miniature white coffin being lowered into the ground as Neil, Sarah, Elizabeth, other friends of Sarah's from church, Sarah's friends from work and Neil's manager all shuddered against a freak late spring flurry of sleet were in the past. The scene of dying daffodils, cherry blossom scattered like confetti on the ground, and the melody of a blackbird cheerfully singing his courtship in a nearby hedge were a distant though still poignant memory. Even the nightmares that followed, the terrible dreams that they had buried Anna alive, rarely troubled him now.

The past year he had found himself avoiding Sarah. Her recriminations and seemingly endless misery depressed him. He'd started volunteering for longer hours at work and increasingly dreaded going home. He was aware that he was in danger of neglecting her, but secretly he thought she should be getting over it. He knew patience wasn't his strongest quality, and he did his best to bite back the criticism and be understanding but he was losing the battle. He felt ready to make a fresh start. He yearned for them to have another baby, but the brooding silences between them seemed to be a permanent way of life, interspersed by rows which were becoming more and more vindictive, and no matter how much they regretted it afterwards things were said that couldn't be taken back.

From today however he hoped all that would change. Today was special. It was a day for optimism and good feelings. He had a surprise for Sarah. He had been told today that he had won promotion to Senior Manager. This meant they could afford to move house. He was sure if only he could get Sarah away from the house where Anna had died, and start in a new home it would make it easier for her to come to terms with the bereavement, and then, surely, she would agree to start a family again. He knew Sarah was reluctant to have another baby. They had
quarreled endlessly over it for the last year, but now he was sure they had the solution within their grasp. In a new environment Sarah was bound to feel differently. He had booked a table at the new Greek restaurant in town so they could celebrate his surprise announcement in style.

CHAPTER TEN

The next few years were to bring about varying degrees of change for each of them.

Elizabeth Lingwood had seen the Community Psychiatric Nurse for six months. She had assiduously practiced the relaxation exercises he taught her, and with his counseling and support she had managed to get to the post box and even to the shops once, but on her own she still rarely left the house. In the end the Community Nurse said there really wasn't anything more he could do for her, and he did have to have an output of clients, so he was very sorry but...he was discharging her. He wouldn't be able to see her anymore. She hadn't been able to leave the house since. For years she was a prisoner in her own house. It seemed implausible now that she had ever been a teacher and travelled the world. She missed her work, her colleagues, her adventures, but nothing on earth could persuade her to step outside her own front door.

***

Mick Hughes had been released from prison after he had finished his sentence, and hadn't been in trouble in the years since but things were tough. Nobody would give an ex-convict a job and money was tight. He did the odd bit of work experience, decorating sheltered accommodation for the elderly organized by a charity that worked with ex-offenders. He also helped Lyndsay with the kids: they had four now, three boys and a girl but most of his time he spent drinking with Terry. Terry was out of work now as well. He'd been sacked from the nightclub when rumour went round that he was beating up his girlfriend. The nightclub owners didn't want that kind of publicity. The girlfriend dumped him at the same time, so he was left with no job and nowhere to live. He had stayed in a hostel until Mick had put a word in for him with his mother-in-law, so Terry had moved into one of Betty Redmond's bedsits.

Right now Terry was sitting in Mick's living room, sprawled in an armchair, swilling his lager around in the can. Mick was in the kitchen making himself a cup of coffee. The kids were sitting at the kitchen table eating their tea and Lyndsay, her face prematurely etched with worry was leaning against the kitchen sink. She'd never liked Terry and stayed out of the way as much as possible when he came round. She swallowed a couple of her anti-depressants with a sip of water.

'Do you have to take those?' Mick asked her.

'They help me. I'm worn out with looking after the kids and scrimping and scraping for money. I feel suicidal. The tablets keep me going.'

'What's suicidal mean Mum?' Rory asked.

'Never you mind. You'll understand it when you're older. How's your sausages?'

'They're nice Mum, thanks.'

'Aren't you going to eat something with the kids?' Mick asked her.

'No. I'm not hungry,' she mumbled.

'You've got to eat something Lynds, look at you, you're nothing but skin and bone, a sparrow eats more than you,' he coaxed. 'You haven't eaten anything all day. Just have a couple of sausages and baked beans same as the kids.'

'The last of the sausages are for you and Terry.'

'We'll get a Chinese takeaway.'

'You'll get a bloody takeaway? I'm trying to save every spare penny. We've got no money to get the kids Xmas presents, and Rory needs new shoes for school.' She regretted her words instantly.

'I'll sort it,' Mick said gruffly.

'No. Don't do anything criminal Mick please. I don't want you getting sent down again. Rory's in school now. The other kids will say things to him if you go to prison and I can't cope on my own. I want you here with me and the kids.' Mick walked over to her and took her in his arms.

'I'm not going to prison again,' he said gently, 'but it's my job to provide for this family. I'll look around again for some casual work, there's sure to be plenty going in the run up to Xmas.' But Lyndsay knew him too well.

'Mick, promise me you won't do anything stupid. I can't go through you being inside again.'

'On my mother's grave I promise.'

'I mean it Mick,' she said firmly, 'you go down again and we're finished. I can't take it. I can't go through that worry again.'

'No worries Lynds, I'll find something legit. I'm not going to do a burglary or anything like that.'
***

Katharine Baines had completed her degree but failed the finals. She had felt too unwell to take re-sits so had come away with nothing. Three years of agonizing stress and worry all for nought. She had tried to crush any feeling of depression when she failed her degree, but she had wanted that qualification so badly, she was hungry for it. She didn't need it just for earning power she needed it for her self esteem.

Afterwards she had got herself a part-time job as a nanny and she and Paul lurched on a bit longer. Then the two children she looked after had started school and nursery so she wasn't needed anymore. Next she got a part-time job in a box office, but got muddled under pressure and gave people the wrong information and she was politely sacked.

Her next job was working as an evening office cleaner but after six months she was so ill, she was talking to herself at work and had to give up work completely. Out of work, stuck at home on her own she was eaten up by anxiety and depression.

Dreams Of Death

CHAPTER ELEVEN

The night Sarah had told Neil she was leaving; he had begged her to stay. He had told her the news about his promotion to Senior Manager convinced it would change her mind but she wouldn't be persuaded.

After Sarah left him he had become very solitary. For a while he carried on with his normal routine, but he felt as though he was just going through the motions. For weeks he held on to the belief that Sarah would come back to him. He talked to her on the phone and wrote to her regularly. Her replies were kind but adamant that she wasn't coming back. As gently as she could, she told him she would be applying for a divorce.

It left Neil a changed man. His last drop of confidence and motivation just seemed to ebb out of him. The breakdown started with the baby's crying. Sitting one evening when there was nothing on the telly before he'd galvanized himself to turn the radio on, just sitting staring into space he heard a baby crying. Not outside, somewhere close. Not any baby, Anna. It was Anna's cry and it wouldn't stop. He put the radio on and drowned it out.

It happened again at work. Staff would be talking to him, but he couldn't hear what they were saying above the noise of the baby crying. He would stare round distractedly looking for the baby, willing its mother to comfort it, to do anything to shut it up. He would cup his hands over his ears, feeling his chest tighten and a cold sweat break out on his forehead. He would see the questioning looks the staff exchanged but he couldn't help himself. His boss had a word with him and suggested he take a couple of weeks off.

At home he got worse. He heard the crying day and night. He couldn't sleep. Hunger pangs gnawed at his stomach but he couldn't eat. He couldn't summon the will to wash, shave, dress, or go back to work. He didn't go out and he stopped answering the door or the phone. Instead he sat in the darkened house, with the curtains drawn day as well as night.

It was his manager, unable to get a reply on the phone from him for weeks on end who drove to the house. The closed curtains convinced him Neil was in and he rang the doorbell non-stop, until Neil gave in and answered the door.

The manager was shocked by Neil's appearance. He was gaunt, unshaven and wearing pyjamas in the middle of the day. Dismayed to find he could get any coherent conversation from Neil, he insisted on calling Neil's family doctor. The doctor called an ambulance to take Neil straight to the psychiatric unit.

Neil was frightened as he was driven to the hospital, but in some corner of his awareness he knew he needed help. He had an image in his mind of clean, pretty wards staffed by gentle female nurses in starched white uniforms. He wasn't sure where he got the idea from, maybe old black and white films. He imagined the nurses sitting with him when he felt distressed, holding his hand and murmuring words of comfort and reassurance.

The psychiatric unit was in the grounds of Bergrove General Hospital. It was the same site where Anna had been born. The unit was accommodated in a small,
modern, grim, grey, concrete building, which had rows and rows of windows like masses of sightless eyes. The ward he was put on was much the same as all the other psychiatric wards. Down the middle ran a long corridor. On the right hand at one end was the men's dormitory. It contained nine beds. Each bed had a wardrobe and cupboard beside it, and a curtain patterned with brown and orange diamonds on a beige background that could be drawn round the bed. At the other end of the corridor on the right was an identical dormitory for women. In between the dormitories were the dining room and sitting room. Someone had made an effort to make the sitting room look homely. It was carpeted instead of the usual hospital lino. It had a telly, sideboard, stereo, armchairs and pictures on the wall. Only the institutional plastic covered armchairs and Cynthia, sitting knitting and muttering furiously to herself, indicated that this was not any ordinary sitting room.

On the other side of the corridor were the nurses' office, the doctors' room, the clinical room, the sluice room and the smoking room. The smoking room was heavily discoloured with nicotine stains, and there was no ventilation. It was a tiny room, and as practically everyone on the ward smoked it was continually crowded. Only those that could get a seat sat round the coffee table, which was covered with overspill from the ash-tray. The rest stood in the doorway flicking ash on the floor.

The male and female nurses wore ordinary clothes. It took Neil several days to work out which people were the staff, and which people were the patients. The patients were good-humoured about it when he thought they were staff, but the staff got very snooty when he thought they were patients. After a few days he realized you could tell the staff from the patients because they wore name badges, but by that time he felt so intimidated by the staff he didn't dare approach them anyway.

Mostly the nurses ignored the patients. Their role consisted of feeding, medicating, telling patients off and holding them down for forced injections. They were open in their contempt for the people in their care.

'Look at him, he's twisted, he's getting worse,' one nurse exclaimed to another, pointing out Neil who was in a very distracted state. The patients around took no notice, they endured such treatment on a daily basis but Neil was shocked and humiliated. The things he saw and heard made him so angry that at times it took every last ounce of self-control he could muster to keep his temper. They had a whole bag of punishments for any patient who dared to challenge them. They could put you under section, increase your medication or withhold treatment, confine you to the ward or even to bed and refuse home leave.

The patients saw very little of the doctors. If you saw a doctor for five minutes once a week you were doing well. The doctors didn't seem to have a clue what went on in the wards, or if they knew they didn't seem to care. One doctor said he thought psychotherapy might help Neil, and that he would refer him but the doctor warned there was a nine month waiting list. When Neil asked how his referral was progressing a few months later, the doctor admitted without apology that he had never actually made the referral.

***

Neil never made a full recovery after that first spell in hospital. After repeated relapses and repeat hospitalizations he had lost his job, his house had been repossessed and his possessions sold. His parents were dead. He had no brothers or sisters. He knew he had relatives somewhere in Scotland, but he didn't know where they lived and had never met them. He thought about going to Elizabeth Lingwood for help, but he didn't know her that well. She had always been Sarah's friend rather than his, and he knew from Sarah's letters that Elizabeth was going through a rough time herself. He thought the last thing she needed was him turning up on her doorstep in his state.

He had trouble getting any benefit money because he had no address to which it could be sent. He spent his days sitting in the public library and his nights huddled in a public lavatory. By a process of trial and error, he discovered that he could get just about enough food, from the remains of takeaways that late night drinkers discarded in the rubbish bins on the High Street. He couldn't however escape the identical barrenness of the days. The unrelenting boredom was unbearable. He remembered the warm comfortable home and loving, lively life he had shared with Sarah before Anna's death, and the poignant contrast with his present circumstances made him wretched.

He thought things couldn't get any worse, until a gang of teenage youths discovered him bedding down in the public lavatory one night.

'It's a tramp,' the first one shouted up the stairs to his mates with disgust. The others rushed down the stairs to gape, all righteous indignation and bristling aggression. Neil saw himself through their eyes: dirty clothes, matted hair and unkempt beard. They blocked the exit so Neil slipped into a cubicle and locked the door for protection.

'You fucking loser we'll have you!' One of them yelled. They hammered and kicked at the door, shouting obscenities and threats. Neil cowered inside staring at the door in fear, expecting it to fall in on him at any moment. He was weak with hunger, shivering and had no energy to fight them off if they got to him. However, after ten minutes of abject terror all went silent. Had they tired of the game or were they waiting for him outside? He stayed in the cubicle all night in case they were still there, but when he risked coming out in the morning they were gone.

After that he wasn't bold enough to venture back to the public lavatory, so he lost his night shelter. He slept in shop doorways but they afforded little protection. The weather was bitter. He huddled up; cupping his fingers over his mouth to catch the warmth of his breath but even his breath was tepid. It was rain he really dreaded. It soaked him through to his underwear. His clothes clung to him cold and clammy, and chafed his skin raw when he moved. It took him days to dry out. He began to think seriously about going to the train station and throwing himself under the express. It was suicide Neil was thinking about; as he sat on a bench in the shopping precinct the next day. He was unable to pluck up the courage to go into the library where he usually spent his days; for fear his slovenly appearance and damp musty smell would offend someone, or the security guard would turf him out. When he heard someone call his name his first thought was that he was hallucinating, but looking up he saw a man a few yards away looking at him and smiling.

It was a man who had been on the same ward as Neil in the psychiatric unit. The man was universally known among the mentally ill community as Chattering John, and was generally avoided partly because of his inability to stop his tongue wagging, but also because of his uncontrollable drinking. Neil had only ever known him when he was on the ward and drying out though, and didn't mind passing time with him.

'I wasn't sure it was you,' John greeted him. I recognized the clothes but you look different..., you look different with a beard,' he ended lamely realizing it would be impolite to comment on Neil's disheveled appearance.

After they had chatted for a few minutes about how life was going for each of them; John invited Neil to go with him to the drop-in for people with mental health problems. Neil had never heard of it before, but was keen to go anywhere out of the rain. He walked stiffly and slowly beside John. It seemed like a lifetime since he'd talked to anyone.

As they walked in through the door of the drop-in, Neil's first impression was of how tatty it looked. The walls were dirty, the formica tables were chipped and cracked, and the mismatched assortment of chairs were torn and ragged. But the warmth, oh god, the wonderful warmth wrapped itself round him like a blanket. Noisy laughter drew Neil's attention to a small group of people sitting at a low table, in the middle of the room. One of them was doing the crossword puzzle in the newspaper, while the others were playing Trivial Pursuits with much banter and jocularity. Neil's heart lifted a little. He craved cheerful company.

The man doing the crossword was plump, had lank fair hair tied back in a pony- tail and a full beard. He looked up.

'What are you doing here?' He barked at John. His lips were drawn back exposing a missing top molar, and he was leaning forward aggressively, his nose wrinkled in a sneer.

'I've got every right to be here,' John replied firmly.

'You know you're not allowed in the drop-in when you're boozed up' the man jeered. John coloured.

'I'm not drunk. I haven't had a drink in twenty-four hours.' The man went back to his newspaper.

'He seems a bit of a rough character,' Neil said to John under his breath.

'That's Joe the assistant manager.' John whispered back. 'All of them at the middle table, they're the staff. The unpaid ones are doing National Vocational Qualifications in Social Care, and come here for their work experience. Two of them have been accepted for psychiatric nurse training. We joke that they're all super-glued to their chairs at that table. The others,' John indicated the forlorn-looking people at the other tables, 'they're the service-users.'

Neil looked round the rest of the room. At the other tables people were sitting either singly or in groups, in silence, most of them staring at the ground. At the nearest table a woman with her hair tied in about ten bunches; each tied with a different coloured ribbon slouched back in her chair. Beside her an elderly woman sat tensely on the edge of her seat. On the other side of the table from them; a man in his twenties with a round prematurely aged face wearing a suit and sitting stiffly upright, rapidly blinked one eye. At the furthest table a middle-aged man hunched in his chair staring intensely into space.

'I stopped taking my medication,' he said to a point in space about two feet ahead of him. 'I haven't slept for eight days. I don't know if I should take my medication.' He repeated the sentences over and over but nobody took any notice of him. Another man with red hair and a beer belly paced the length of the room.

'This is a fucking shit-hole isn't it?' He asked of nobody in particular. Joe stopped doing his crossword and looked up again.

'You don't have to come here if you don't like it,' he chuckled.

John showed Neil the kitchen, and they waited in the queue to make themselves a cup of tea. The woman using the tea urn turned round and John introduced her to Neil.

'This is Katharine. Katharine Baines. She has just been using the drop-in a short time and she's the woman I'm determined to marry.' John dropped to one knee holding his hands in a pleading gesture. 'Will you marry me Katharine?' He said heartily.

'I'm afraid not John,' she smiled shyly. She nodded a hello to Neil, and took her mug of tea and went into the main room.

'It's hopeless John. Give it up. She's way out of your league,' said a slim dark-haired man eating beans on toast at the kitchen table.

'I know. She's too good for me really, and too good for the likes of this place,' John replied.

'Martin's off to Sydney for the amateur World Chess Championships next week,' the blond man sitting on the other side of the table joined in.

'Good on you,' John responded.

'Now steady on, you'll give me a big head,' Martin said with exaggerated coyness.

'He came third in the world last year,' his friend added. Martin blushed.

After they had got their tea Neil and John went back into the main room.

'Is he really a chess champion?' Neil asked John.

'Oh yes. He plays every year. He spends the year taking part in amateur tournaments, and if he does well enough in the tournaments he qualifies for the World Championship. Bit of a brain box. He went to private school. Can't work or anything now. His depression's too bad but he's got a generous grandfather who pays his air fares so he can take part in the Championship.'

Neil sat down at the middle table. He wanted to be with people who had some life about them, but he sat well away from Joe. John hesitated and then rather nervously sat next to Neil. One of the men playing Trivial Pursuits looked up and stared hard at Neil.

'What's your name?' The man asked.

'Neil.'

'And your last name?'

'Soames.' The man wrote Neil's name down in the attendance book and went back to playing Trivial Pursuits. That was the last word any of the staff spoke to Neil until the drop-in closed a couple of hours later.

At one point Joe called across to Katharine: 'Are you going out with John yet?'

'No,' she replied flushing red.

'You never go out with anyone. You belong in a fucking nunnery!' Joe taunted.

Neil was appalled. 'Don't talk to her like that,' he scolded Joe. Joe scowled at him but appeared to think better of saying anything, and went back to his paper.

As they walked back to town together John filled Neil in on some of the detail about the drop-in and its occupants.

'Martin who plays chess, his mother died of cancer when he was seven and his step-father was a tyrant. Adam, his friend, who was sitting opposite him, never gives away anything personal. He's a bit of a rough diamond, but his hearts in the right place. Sandra, the woman with her hair in bunches, her mother was scalded to death in a bath in an accident at her retirement home, and her father developed Alzheimer's disease and wandered off and was found dead in a ditch. Laura, the elderly woman sitting beside Sandra, her husband moved his girlfriend into their house while Laura was still living there. Laura does a bit of voluntary work for the charity Age Concern. Tim, the man who blinks with one eye all the time, has learning disabilities as well as mental health problems. The young man who was saying he hadn't taken his medication I don't know. I haven't seen him in the drop-in before.'

'Joe, the assistant manager is a nasty piece of work. He can turn on the charm at first especially with women, but sooner or later he turns nasty on everyone. He gets a kick out of hurling abuse and winding everybody up. He seems to particularly dislike quiet people. We used to have a volunteer worker Steve, a quiet, pleasant bloke who didn't sit at the table with the staff group but played pool with the service users. Joe used to try and goad Steve into losing his temper. Joe would make derogatory remarks about Steve's quietness and appearance, although he wore perfectly ordinary jeans and t-shirt.'

'Joe would be going go on, swear at me, you haven't got the bottle have you?' And all this kind of stuff trying to provoke him, he was dead serious. Steve always ignored him. He put up with it for ages but in the end he left.'

'Katharine is quite quiet and self-contained as well so Joe's starting to have a go at her. Joe knows I've got a huge crush on her so he interferes. He started out being sweet as pie to her trying to persuade her to go out with me, but I know I've no chance really. I've talked to Katharine and she says she is desperate to get away from the place, but like the rest of us she's got nowhere else to go.'

By now John and Neil were back in the town centre. It had stopped raining and they sat on Neil's bench outside the library. John prattled on.

'Then there was the time Joe went to the pub after work with a group of service users from the drop-in. Joe got drunk and ended up smacking one of them in the face, because it happened outside the drop-in and outside working hours nobody did anything about it.' Neil listened with growing dismay.

'It doesn't sound much like the literature I read on the notice-board which says the drop-in provides a comfortable, relaxed atmosphere in which staff raise users' confidence and self-esteem,' he remarked.

'The drop-in was founded and is run on a philosophy of self-help and unstructured non-activity,' John continued. 'What that means translated into reality is that there's sod all to do, and everybody's going nuts through sheer boredom and no matter how ill you are the staff won't lift a finger to help you. We've pleaded with the manager to change it, but he just tells us to shut up he doesn't want to hear about it. They had two women from the drop-in jump to their deaths from neighbouring tower blocks within a few weeks of each other in the summer. They had both tried to get help from the drop-in shortly before they jumped.'

'But you still go there?' Neil asked curiously. John sighed heavily and pulled a long face.

'I share supported housing with people I don't like. I'm desperate to get a break from them. I'd go to the Welland Road day-centre, but the woman I share with goes there and I want to get away from her. I've asked to go to the Linden Street day centre but they won't take me till I've sorted out my alcohol problems.' For a few moments they sat in silence. John turned to Neil and patted him on the arm.

'Look, Neil, I'm really sorry I can't help you with accommodation,' he said 'but in supported housing you're not allowed overnight visitors. If they found out I'd let you stay I could lose my tenancy.'

'It's alright, don't worry about it' Neil reassured him. They said their good-byes. After John had gone Neil sat brooding. He must keep his mind focused on the positive he told himself. He had found a place to go during the day that was warm and dry, where he could get a hot drink and where he didn't feel out of place. He would just have to try and ignore the bad stuff.

For the next few weeks Neil took to going to the drop-in daily. The same routine continued in the drop-in day in and day out, week after week occasionally punctuated by outbursts of aggression from Joe. The manager was seldom seen but
a few times he passed through the drop-in staring at everyone with steely eyes, and then closeted himself in the office for the rest of the day.

Neil talked to John when he was in and got to know Martin and his friend Adam and Katharine. At first Katharine listened but didn't say much. Gradually though she started to come out of her shell, and she and Neil had some good chats. It was with great pleasure that Neil discovered that they had the same sense of humour. There were times when he found himself laughing for the first time in a very long while, and then Katharine stopped coming. Nobody knew where she lived or what had happened to her. It was a surprise to Neil to realize how much he missed her.

Then John stopped coming in as well. Rumour had it that he was on another drinking binge. Neil tried to talk to the other people using the drop-in but they didn't have much to say. He struck lucky though when one of them told him about Newhaven House; a local day centre for the homeless.

The next day Neil went along to the day-centre. It was a big old house which at first sight was rather bleak and unwelcoming. Inside everything was very basic. The floors were bare wood, but you could have a hot bath, use the washing machine and dryer for a pound, there were free mugs of tea, and you could have a cooked dinner for fifty pence.

After his first bath in two months the place didn't seem so bleak. Neil got himself a mug of tea and sat down. There were at least twenty people there; mostly men but a couple of women as well. From listening to the conversations going on around him; it seemed that most of them had mental health problems. The staff were fairly patronizing but at least they took an interest. After asking Neil about his situation; one of them gave him the address of a local voluntary organization that helped homeless people find accommodation.

Neil went to the organization's office straight away, and by nightfall they had got him a room in a hostel. Neil cursed his naiveté and clouded thinking for not realizing there would be such places when he had first left hospital, but he was a newcomer to life on the underbelly of society. He was only slowly learning its way of functioning.

The hostel was in a fourteen-storey tower block, and Neil's room was on the top floor. The room was small but it had a bed and a wash basin and was heated. Neil was relieved and delighted beyond words to be spending the night somewhere out of the wind and rain. As he was closing the curtains he paused. The view showed the whole of the town, and in the distance below the street lamps looked like twinkling fairy lights. Maybe it was a sign he thought; an omen that things were going to get better. When he got into bed he tucked the blankets closely round him and sank against the mattress. Relaxation suffused his body. He hadn't realized till now just how stiff and achy he had got from being tensed against the rough weather; while sleeping on concrete paths during his nights outdoors. Sleeping in a bed again was heavenly bliss.

The hostel provided three meals a day and the food was excellent; ten times better than hospital food and plenty of it. The downside was the continuing boredom of hostel life and the other residents. For the most part they were tough, hard-faced young men who uniformly referred to the residents with mental health problems as 'cabbages'. It was in his second week at the hostel that one of them mugged him.

Neil came out of his room and started walking down the short corridor to the landing where the lifts were. A man appeared at the end of the corridor. He stood still staring at Neil briefly then his glance darted away and he walked slowly towards Neil. Neil hesitated. Although the man was no longer paying any attention to him there was a tension in the man's posture; a studied effort in his diverted gaze that set Neil's alarm bells ringing. Neil tried to take stock. The man would reach him before he could get back to his room. There was nothing he could do to avoid the man, but he balled his fists in readiness and made his stride more purposeful. At the same time though a part of his mind told him he was being silly, that this was just paranoia striking yet again. Maybe it was this distrust of his own judgment which caused him to be taken by surprise; despite his premonition of danger when the attack eventually came.

The man drew level with him and passed him and Neil slackened his fists and mentally relaxed. As Neil was rebuking himself for his irrational fears a hand flashed in front of his face; grabbed him by the throat in an iron grip and slammed him back against the wall. The assailant stood close to Neil their chests touching. Neil looked up at him. He could feel the man's breath on his face and see a nerve twitching at the corner of his eye.

'Give me your wallet' the man said almost coaxingly. The only money Neil had for the next week was in his wallet, and his only picture of Anna. Neil tensed his muscles ready to fight back but as he tried to think of a plan of attack; the man suddenly jerked him forward by the throat and slammed him back again banging Neil's head hard against the wall.

'I'll use the fucking knife on you' the man rasped. It was only then that Neil noticed the itchy pressure against his cheek. He nearly soiled himself.

There was nothing he could do. The man was bigger than him, stronger than him and armed. They were on the fourteenth floor of the tower block where only two or three tenants had rooms, and even if any of them did happen across the scene they would probably look the other way and pretend they hadn't seen anything. The few staff were on the ground floor and there was no way to alert them. As Neil reached for his wallet; he saw suspicion flit across the man's face and his grip round Neil's throat tightened. Neil gulped for breath.

'I'm just getting my wallet' he implored hoarsely. The man released his grip on Neil's throat to take the wallet. As the man edged away Neil saw the Stanley knife in the man's hand. Perplexed, he saw the glistening blood on its blade, and then started to feel his cheek stinging.

'You come after me or you say a word to anyone and next time it won't be your face I cut, it'll be your throat,' the man threatened. The man backed away to the end of the corridor and disappeared round the corner.

Neil stood rooted to the spot for a few moments and then ran back to his room. In the mirror he could see a scarlet scratch on his cheek oozing beads of blood, which dribbled down his face and hung in drips on his jaw line. He cleaned himself up at the basin, and sat for several hours pressing a wad of tissue to the cut to stop it bleeding, afraid to leave his room.

At last he forced himself to go downstairs. He checked inside the lifts and scoured every inch of the thirteen flights of stairs; hoping the man might just have taken his cash and discarded his wallet. On the ground floor he was rewarded. He found his wallet empty of cash and his benefits book but, with Anna's picture still in it.

He passed the staff office but didn't go in to report the attack for fear of retaliation from the man or his mates. He steeled himself to go into the dining room which was nearly full. There were about forty people in the room, and as he scanned the room looking for the mugger everybody in the room seemed to look back at him with the face of his attacker.

When he told them about the attack at the drop-in Joe perked up.

'You're a born fucking victim,' he snarled. 'You'll always be a victim; you'll be mugged over and over again.' Neil resolved then and there not to use the drop-in again. He could never relax there. There was always tension in the air. He had his room at the hostel now and without Katherine or John for company there was no point really going to the drop-in anymore.

He told himself that he just had to forget about the attack, and get on with his life but for weeks afterwards he had a recurring dream that he was running down the corridor naked, scared, and knocking on the doors of the neighbouring rooms. No-one answered. He would see a man coming towards him swinging a knife at his throat, and then as the knife was just about to strike he woke up. He would be sweating; have a throbbing headache and the healing cut on his cheek would tingle and itch, as if the wound was reopened by the memory. It had taken over a month for the dreams to stop, and for him to stop feeling skittish every time one of the other residents came near him, but he never saw his attacker again and gradually the nervousness subsided.

***

No longer having to cope with the deprivation and degradation of living on the streets, at last on regular benefits, and away from the demoralizing influence of the drop-in, Neil's mental health began to improve. He felt more motivated and confident and he made enquiries about getting permanent council accommodation. He was told he would normally be on the waiting list for years before he got an offer of housing, but if he was prepared to take a hard to let bedsit in Canley End the roughest, most derelict area of Bergrove, they could offer him something straight away.

Neil was desperate enough to consider it and went to have a look at a bedsit. The
bedsit was tiny and run down in a block of flats with boarded up windows on the bottom floor, and a row of drug dealers openly plying their trade outside the front door. Neil had a long think about taking the bedsit. He was eager to get out of the hostel, but he knew he would feel constantly threatened in Canley End. He would be afraid to go outside his front door. He was paranoid enough without living in an environment that was known for being a hotbed of trouble. He

turned down the council's offer and started looking for private accommodation.

It took him several months, but eventually he was able to sort himself out a place in a reasonably cheap but safe area. It bucked him up no end. He felt quite well and enthusiastic. He went out and got himself part-time voluntary work as an assistant youth worker; as a step towards getting back into paid full-time employment. It was challenging working with teenagers, but he got buckets of self-esteem from feeling he was doing something useful again. He really started to feel like life could be good once more.

Then there was an incident with the youngsters. Neil and another youth worker took a group of lads on an evening swimming trip to a leisure centre, but they got lost on route and by the time they got there the pool was closed. The lads vented their frustration on the way back by slashing the seats of the minibus. Neil had been in the back of the minibus with them but had been unable to stop them. Although nobody blamed him for what had happened he felt responsible.

He lost all confidence in himself and started finding the work very stressful. His anxiety levels went through the ceiling to the point where he couldn't function anymore, and he had to give up the voluntary work. This made him severely depressed. He felt like a failure. When the form came through the post for him to renew his housing benefit; he couldn't get his head together to fill it in. He put it to one side and forgot about it. They stopped paying his housing benefit. He got into rent arrears and was evicted. He ended up back on the streets, then in the hostel, then a spell in the psychiatric unit, the whole soul-destroying cycle all over again.

Dreams Of Death

CHAPTER TWELVE

It was November nineteen ninety-five and Elizabeth Lingwood was sitting by the window yet again when the second post came. There was only one letter in the post and it was from Sarah Soames. She was writing to tell Elizabeth of her forthcoming wedding. She was marrying an older man, she wrote, a widower in his fifties. Despite the age difference between them she thought they would do well together. He was a kind man and wouldn't expect her to have children; as he already had two grown-up children of his own. She had decided she would never have any more children as a penance for having taken the life of her first child, and forfeiting the life of her second. It was the only way she could put her conscience at ease and allow herself happiness with her new husband to be. She wrote about the wedding plans and incidental anecdotes, and ended by asking if Elizabeth had heard any news of Neil as she had received no word from him since he signed the divorce papers. Elizabeth lay the letter down. She hoped at long last Sarah would have peace of mind and happiness, but she would be able to tell her nothing of Neil when she replied. She had heard nothing of him for years.

She looked out of the window, leaned forward and pressed the palm of her hand hard against the window pane, trying to feel some contact with a world she couldn't join. As she took her hand away she saw a white van. From time to time over the past few weeks she had noticed this white van parked along the road. The driver never got out – just sat for a while before driving off. Elizabeth didn't recognise him as one of the local residents who regularly passed her window, and she had begun to grow suspicious. She decided to ring the police. By the time the police arrived the van had gone. She gave them a description of the van and the driver but the van had been at the wrong angle for her to see the registration number. The police seemed pretty indifferent to her information, but told her to ring them straight away if she saw the van again. She hoped she wouldn't. It was starting to play on her nerves.

***

Lyndsay Redmond stood in her back garden with her baby son in her arms. Next to her was her mother Betty. Her two young sons and daughter, stood in front of her stamping their feet and blowing on their hands.

'The kids are freezing' Betty said 'where the hell is their Dad? He said he had the fireworks all set up ready.' At that point a figure bounded through the garden gate wearing a cape, a long, curling, false moustache, a feathered hat and a plastic sword at his side. Lyndsay's little girl let out a shriek.

'Ah – ha! I am the dastardly Guy Fawkes come to blow up the Houses of Parliament,' their thinly disguised father bellowed.

'Mick,' Lyndsay remonstrated half-heartedly, with affectionate exasperation.

'I spy me a pretty wench,' Mick roared, whacking Lyndsay on the backside with his plastic sword.

'Don't! I'll drop the baby,' she chided.

'I am off to do the deadly deed, let all ye standing here be my witnesses,' and he scampered down the garden and lit the first firework. It exploded into the sky in a burst of green and purple flashes. Mick cheered and the children joined in and clapped. The next firework was gold and silver. The one after let off a succession of ear-splitting bangs that made the baby cry so Lyndsay had to take him indoors.

Half an hour later the fireworks were all gone and the family went inside for burgers and cocoa.

'While I'm here, I want a word with you Mick,' Betty demanded. 'Your mate Terry is behind with his rent again. I spoke to him about it this morning and he gave me a mouthful of abuse. I want you to speak to him. I want my rent money and I don't want him using that kind of language to me again.' Behind her back Mick rolled his eyes. The children giggled and Betty looked around suspiciously.

'Ok Bet, I'll have a word,' Mick told her trying to keep his face straight. 'But you know they're behind with paying his housing benefit, it's not his fault.'

'I don't give a fig whose fault it is. He's not staying in my house for nothing,' she said sharply. 'I told him this morning if he doesn't come up with some rent in the next couple of weeks I'm kicking him out.

When Mick had seen Betty home he popped upstairs to Terry's room.

The old girl tells me you gave her a bit of a mouthful today,' Mick laughed. Terry said nothing but threw him a can of lager. Mick sat down, opened his can, took a sup and leaned close to Terry.

'Look Tez I've got a suggestion. You need some cash fast; Lyndsay and I need some extra money to spend on the kids. I'm planning a job. I've been keeping an eye on this posh house over on Earlsham Park. But I'll need some help with it. If you want a slice of the action I'll cut you in fifty-fifty. I know a good fence. What d'you say?'

The scowl slipped from Terry's face. 'I'm in mate,' he answered, 'just tell me when.'

It was eight o'clock when Betty Redmond woke up the next morning. As she put on her dressing gown and slippers; her breath turned to steam in the cold air. She went into the living room and turned the gas fire on full blast. The flames at the bottom of the fire which normally burnt blue were burning yellow and orange. She carried on to the kitchen and put the kettle on, then went to the hall door, pulling the draught excluder out of the way, unlocked the door and stepped into the hall to pick up the post from the doormat. She shuffled through the letters, left the tenants' post on the ledge and went back into the living room with her own mail. She pushed the door shut, and jammed the draught excluder hard against the bottom of the door to shut out the cold air she could feel coming from underneath.

With her letter tucked in her dressing gown pocket, she went back to the kitchen and made herself a cup of coffee and put slices of bread in the toaster. She took her coffee and shutting the kitchen door behind her pulled her chair up close to the fire in the living room and sat down. She yawned and stretched. God she was tired. She'd woken at three in the morning, and tossed and turned till at least six before she could get back to sleep. She felt as though she could do with another couple of hours in bed. She opened her letter. It was a final notice warning her that her gas supply would be disconnected if she didn't pay the bill imminently. She propped it on the mantelpiece. Thank god she had a new tenant coming in she thought; else with one tenant in arrears and another room empty she wouldn't be able to pay the bill. Her fingers and toes tingled as they began to warm up. There was a bang as the light bulb blew, throwing the room into sudden darkness. She couldn't be bothered to change it just now. She hoped she wasn't going down with anything. She'd been feeling a bit like she had the flu the past few days. She settled back in her chair. The clock on the mantelpiece ticked mesmerically. She thought her toast would be going cold but she didn't want to leave the comfort of the fire. Her eye-lids began to feel heavy. Warm, relaxed doziness suffused her. Her head nodded gently against her chest, and her grip on her cup of coffee loosened. The fire continued to pump out its carbon monoxide fumes.

***

Katharine Baines' son Paul was just thirteen now and at secondary school. He was still struggling to get on at school but he had become an army cadet. It was something he had decided to do on his own initiative and he was good at it. He won awards and he was committed. He might find every excuse to avoid going to school, but if Katharine couldn't afford his bus fare he would walk five miles to get to cadets. Katharine was bemused by how well he accepted the discipline but was mostly thrilled that he had found something purposeful to do. She bought him bits of kit and encouraged him as much as she could, not that he needed it. She was keen for him to stay on course and make a success of it, but she had a niggling worry. She worried that the IRA would blow up his base while Paul was there. Initially she tried to dismiss her anxiety. She'd always been a worrier. As time went on however the worry didn't diminish. It became more and more of a conviction. She started to have visions, visions of herself frantically searching through the bombed out rubble of the base for her son. The visions always ended the same way. She found Paul's mangled lifeless body. It tormented her unbearably.

As if that wasn't enough she began to have the feeling that her sister who had emigrated to Australia was going to be murdered. When she read in the paper that two hitchhikers had been found dead at Alice Springs; she was convinced one of them was her sister. On another occasion there was a news report that a gunman had run amok shooting people in Melbourne. Although Katharine's sister lived in Sydney, she sometimes visited friends in Melbourne, and again Katharine was beside herself with fear that her sister had been killed. She couldn't afford to ring Australia so would write to her sister on the slightest pretext, and wait on tenterhooks for a reply that would let her know her sister was still alive.

She expected every knock at the door to be the police informing her of the death of her son or her sister. The constant anxiety was like a parasite that gnawed away at her sanity and energy, until she felt uncontrollably mad and helplessly exhausted.

With time it gradually dawned on Katharine that she was psychic. No matter how many times her fears were disproved she knew now without a doubt that she was having clairvoyant experiences, and it would just be a matter of time before her dreadful premonitions came true. The terror she felt with these delusions was indescribable. She sat in trance-like reveries for hours at a time totally absorbed in her imagination. She started sleeping up to eighteen hours a day. She became disorientated. Time seemed to lose all meaning. She didn't know what day it was. She tried to send Paul to school on a Saturday. Her watch would say five o' clock and she wouldn't know whether that meant morning or evening.

Once or twice in a glimmer of lucidity she thought she should make an appointment to see the doctor, but the thought was forgotten within moments. Paul heated up a bowl of soup for her and she thought he had poisoned it. In the end she couldn't contain what was going on any longer. She told Paul in a rush of hysterical tears that she feared she was going mad, and he went to the phone box and called the doctor out. Within an hour she had been admitted to a ward at the Psychiatric unit. Paul was taken into foster care since there were no other relatives to look after him. Her life had hit rock bottom of a downward spiral that had lasted for years. It felt like there would never be a way up again.

Dreams Of Death

CHAPTER THIRTEEN

Neil was back on Nairn ward in the psychiatric unit. He had been in many times over the previous five years, and he doubted this time would be his last, but he was an old hand now. He knew the limitations. He had no illusions left. No false expectations. He didn't let them raise his hopes anymore only to dash them. He kept his head down and took everything they said with a large measure of skepticism. They saw he was fed and medicated when he was too ill to do it for himself, but no tablets could substitute for his need for the warm emotional support, and interest of another human being. He had seen Katharine Baines arrive on the ward and they had exchanged a few words, but she seemed quite ill and withdrawn and they hadn't really talked.

It was midmorning the day after fireworks night and he was feeling unwell. He had overheard the nurses having a conversation yesterday and it had left him deeply distressed.

'Did you hear about Chattering John?' One of them had asked the others.

'No. What's he done now?'

'Is he in detox again?' They asked.

'No, he's dead. Threw himself under a train at the railway station last week.'

'Oh well. He was a bloody nuisance anyway,' and they all nodded their heads in agreement.

Today all Neil's senses felt heightened. Colours were intensely vivid and jangled on his nerves. Every sound seemed terrifically loud and dinned in his ears. Since he had woken up that morning, the voices had been bothering him.

'Little bastard' they hissed at him. 'Rotten apple' they taunted, 'rotten to the core' they spat inside his head. He banged the sides of his head hard with his fists but the voices only laughed. 'You want to face up to yourself' they jeered. 'Take a long hard look in the mirror, rotten little bastard, rotten little bastard.' Their sneers echoed relentlessly in his head. He just wanted to go back to bed; put his Walkman on full blast and drown them out, but he couldn't go back to bed he had things to do.

Tracy, an excitable young woman in her early twenties was in the smoking room on the ward shouting at the top of her voice, 'I'm going back on the roads, I'm going back on the fucking roads.' The other occupants of the smoking room paused briefly to digest this piece of behavior then cast their eyes back down to study the carpet, and resumed puffing on their cigarettes. Gerald, the Charge Nurse who was the nearest member of staff to the smoking room rushed to the room, pulled the two patients standing in the doorway out of the way, wordlessly grabbed Tracy's arm, twisted it up behind her back and started to push her towards the women's dormitory. Another male nurse joined him in the corridor and grabbed Tracy's other arm. Neil watched silently as they manhandled her into the dormitory. He hated seeing the other patients restrained, and Tracy was a sectioned patient and could be forcibly injected. He knew from past experience she wouldn't submit without a fight, and he didn't want to be around to see an ever-increasing number of nurses piling on top of her and holding her down screaming. As Neil approached the ward door, Katharine Baines came in carrying a fruit loaf.

'I've been baking in Occupational Therapy. It's for my son's birthday. He's visiting me this afternoon' she told Neil with shy pride.

'What is that?' The nursing assistant mocked. 'It's all sunk in the middle. It looks like a brick. You could build a house with that.'

'Take it away, it stinks, it's stinking the place out,' the other nurse added. Katharine moved away. Neil walked up to the nurses.

'What did you have to talk to her like that for?' He asked angrily. 'You're supposed to be encouraging her.'

'We were just raising her self-awareness,' the nursing assistant said in a peeved tone.

'And any more of that attitude from you and I think we'll have to give you an injection,' the staff nurse said. As a voluntary patient they had no right to inject Neil against his will, but he knew it only took a bad report from the nurses and the doctor might section him. He didn't dare say anymore.

Neil wanted to get away from the scene as quickly as possible, and he didn't want anyone to stop him for a chat so he hurried down the stairs, along the corridor, past the coffee bar, through the reception area and out the front door. The sky was glassy. Neil imagined if you held a lighted match to it the sky would melt and ooze washed-out powder blue globules; over the brown roofs of the surrounding houses. It was too cold to dawdle so he walked briskly by the anonymous nondescript building that somebody had once told him was the mortuary, past the incineration plant with the small, staccato puffs of smoke issuing from its chimney and on to the general hospital. He skirted round the ambulances herded at the entrance, averting his eyes from the stretchers with their red-blanketed occupants. He faintly registered the array of faces in the waiting room, variously bored, anxious, resigned, and impatient and hurried across the waiting room and into the lift.

There was only one other person in the lift, a middle-aged woman, glaring through her spectacles, her mouth fixed in a permanent sneer of disdain. She was wearing a badge and holding a bundle of case notes. She was probably a ward clerk Neil thought. He wrung his hands. He was always afraid someone would demand to know what he was doing here although nobody had ever challenged him yet.

He got out on the fifth floor and walked down the corridor and into the chapel. It was a big room. It had a plush red carpet and sixteen long pews with wooden backs and green plastic seats. The wooden altar and pulpit stood on a raised platform. On the wall behind the altar hung a large, plain, bronze cross. Dotted around the room were displays of artificial flowers, white lilies on a wooden stand, pink and mauve chrysanthemums and roses in a vase on top of the piano, and unidentifiable salmon pink flowers and green plastic ferns on a shelf on the wall. All along the outside wall was a stained glass window in a multicoloured abstract design. It blocked the natural light, and made the room dim, but an overhead light lit up the altar like a beam of sunshine. The room had an aura that was stagnant and sterile, but it was peaceful. This was Neil's secret sanctuary.

Neil had first found the chapel by chance. One time when he was having a psychotic spell he had been convinced he would find Anna alive on the children's ward. In his search for the children's ward he had come across the chapel. Since then he came here regularly whenever he was in the psychiatric unit. He didn't come for any religious reason, but when it was more bedlam than asylum on the ward, or when he was feeling particularly bad himself this was his private retreat.

The nurses' treatment of Tracy and Katharine had disturbed him, and he sat for a while just hugging himself and rocking backwards and forwards, but the quiet of the chapel helped to soothe him a little, and after a while he walked over to the window. If he got really close to it he could see through the colour to the outside world. Over the road he could see the maternity unit where Anna had been born. A couple of toy town cars drove past and he could see a few small figures scurrying around on the ground. He had a sense of being wonderfully remote and distant. He felt secure in this room on his own. He heard clicking footsteps approach the chapel and looked up expecting to see someone come in, but whomever it was carried on walking down the corridor and their footsteps died away. He thought about Sarah and Anna. When he was stressed or ill he often had memory problems. He would think back and it would be blank. He could remember his name and address and that sort of thing but the events of his life were all jumbled up and incomplete. Eventually the memories would come back but to have forgotten Sarah and the baby at all seemed like a betrayal. These were the two people he had loved most in his entire life. It broke his heart that he would never see or hear or touch either of them again. Now he loved no-one and no-one loved him, and he knew that was how it would be for the rest of his life. It was a heart-ache that never entirely left him.

Checking his watch he realized he had to go. He had an important errand to run. He didn't feel up to going to town today but he couldn't put it off. He made his way downstairs, and shuffled to the bus stop shaking his head from side to side trying to dislodge the insults ricocheting inside his skull.

As he stood at the bus stop over the road from the general hospital; he experienced a sort of vertigo. He kept getting the sensation that he was going to fall into the road. He took a few steps backwards further away from the kerb, but he still felt as though he was going to fall in front of a car. He shuffled a few more steps backwards and then a few more, until he was standing on the grass verge behind the path.

Two young men wearing the standard uniform of their sex and age group, jeans, trainers, long jumpers and leather jackets, watched Neil curiously. One arched an eyebrow theatrically and the other sniggered uneasily. A woman with a sagging, wrinkled face retained an inscrutable gaze looking Neil straight in the eye. Beside her an Asian woman wearing a thick brown winter coat over a gold and cream coloured sari, firmly unclasped the hands of the toddler hugging her legs, and gently pushing the child ahead of her edged surreptitiously further away from Neil. He was embarrassed by the consternation he'd caused.

Neil was relieved when he finally got to sit securely in a seat on the bus. As the journey to town progressed however, he began to feel faint. He often had these spells. He thought maybe it was a side-effect of the medication but the doctor said it was anxiety. His head spun so badly and he felt so sick; that he had to lie down on the seat so he didn't collapse. Lying down helped and by the time the bus reached town his head felt considerably clearer. As he walked to his next stop he popped into the newsagents to scan the front page headlines of the papers. It was his habit to check the headlines to keep up with some idea of what was going on in the world. He didn't like watching television, at best he found it hard to follow, at worst he thought it was giving him cryptic messages. The only radio on the ward was in the smoking room, and as he didn't smoke he didn't want to be in the stuffy atmosphere. His concentration and memory were too poor to read a paper all through. By the time he got to the end of a sentence he had forgotten the beginning of it so it made no sense to him, but he could manage just the headlines. Today the newspapers in their own styles were all carrying the same front page story. 'Psycho-killer Let Loose by Doctors,' 'Schizophrenic Slays Innocents,' 'Community Care Killer Caught by Police,' 'Maniac Freed to Murder.' Neil felt guilty and ashamed by association. He cringed with a deep sense of disgust and self-loathing.

He continued to the next bus stop where he had to wait twenty minutes for his connecting bus. He stood with his back pressed against a shop window for support and the cool air helped refresh him. He smelt the heady scent of flowers and realized he was standing in front of a flower shop. Next to him the front of the shop was open and every type of flower obtainable in the November season was on display. He had a flashback to the Summer when this last bout of illness had begun. He could remember the moment he had first felt the tiny germ of madness needling his consciousness from the deepest recesses of his brain. It had been a fleeting moment and he had refused to acknowledge it, but it had returned and over the weeks the madness had seeped through every furrow and connected with every nerve in his brain. He had been almost completely incapacitated; at the mercy of every twitch and spasm of the chaos swirling in his head. He'd shut himself in his room making only brief trips to the shop once a week for baked beans and bread.

That's when he had noticed the flowers in the gardens he'd passed. He hadn't taken in what they looked like. Everything around him had seemed alien and unreachable but the smell of the flowers, warm, sweet and familiar had found its way inside his veiled world. He'd bought a bunch of flowers, and taken them home with him believing it would help to have something in his room that elicited a positive response from his senses, but when he'd got them home they'd had no scent.

His disappointment had been furious. It seemed like a sign of the futility of putting up any fight against his illness. Sitting, tears of frustration rolling down his
cheeks, his attention had been caught by a patch of sunlight on the carpet. The sun's rays were forming a spotlight. He'd got down on the floor on his hands and knees and closing his eyes had arched his back to let the streaming sunlight bathe his face.   Strange, coloured shapes had danced in front of his eyes against the back drop of an orange glow. When his eyes started to ache he had curled himself small so that his whole body was contained in the circle of sunshine, and had lain down to rest his head. The sun warmed his tear-stained cheek. He could feel the steady thud of his heart and hear the soft sigh of his breath. He felt the tension go out of his body and his mind quieted. Was this what it was like in the womb he wondered? He thought that if he could stay cocooned in this beam of sunshine to the end of his life he would never be troubled again. His psyche was at peace, but after half an hour the sun had shifted and he began to grow cold. His muscles ached, he got pins and needles from the pressure of the hard floor, and the carpet prickled against his skin making him itch. Those precious

moments of relaxation of body and mind were gone and he felt insanity fasten its grip once more. Was he better now? The doctors thought so but he wasn't so sure. Sometimes it was hard to tell. He wasn't sure he could remember what 'well' should feel like anymore.

His musings were interrupted by the arrival of his bus. On this leg of his bus journey he was able to sit up normally. He watched the neat, glamorous shops, and the carefully positioned artificial trees, hanging baskets and fountains of the town centre give way to tatty little shops, boarded up buildings and industrial units. He thought whoever named this area Greenstead must have had a sense of irony. Wherever you looked was dusty, grimy yellow, grey or brown, but perhaps it had been green here once.

He carefully checked the names of all the side roads as the bus passed. He'd forgotten to bring his street map with him, but could remember that Marlborough Road was the last turn off on the left before his stop. He had made this journey yesterday. He had been to see a bedsit; they were discharging him from the hospital in two weeks. The landlady had introduced herself as Betty Redmond. She was a short, heavy set woman with short dark brown hair and thick-rimmed glasses that seemed to magnify the piercing gaze of her eyes. She didn't smile. Neil had explained that he had come about the room to let advertised in the paper, and she had taken him upstairs to see it. She had pointed out the shower cubicle on the first floor, the toilet, and the 'kitchen', a cooker and a sink unit at the end of the corridor. She told him the front door was always left unlocked but he would have his own key to his room, and then she opened a chocolate brown door which had dents in the bottom where somebody had obviously kicked it. She left him to look round the room on his own and told him she would be in her flat downstairs.

The room was the usual sort of thing for what a social security tenant could get. It was decorated with wallpaper that had cream coloured flowers on a brown background. It made the room look dark and dingy. In patches mould obliterated the cream flowers. The ceiling was stained an ochre colour. The only furniture was a single bed, a wardrobe and an old-fashioned dressing table. Neil tried to ignore the stained mattress on the bed; so worn in places the stuffing was showing. Most of the floor area was covered with a threadbare grey carpet with a pattern of faded pink flowers, but dust covered linoleum framed the edges.

Well, he thought, if he could get some fungicidal spray he could clean the mould off the walls. If the landlady would let him decorate, he could paint it in something light-coloured, cheer it up a bit. With the aid of a step-ladder he could wash the ceiling. A new mattress and carpet to finish it off, and it wouldn't be too bad at all. Then he sighed. What was he thinking of? He had his head in the clouds. His benefit money didn't last the week just buying basics. He wasn't going to be able to do anything to the room. He'd just have to live in it as it was. He didn't have enough time or money to be choosy.

Neil went back downstairs. The door to Betty Redmond's flat was open. As Neil walked into her living room, the humid warmth tickled the back of his throat. Damp laundry was steaming on a clothes-horse in front of a gas fire which vibrated noisily. He felt nervous about interrupting her. He lost all his assertiveness when he was acutely ill. Betty stood at the work top in her kitchen with her back to him. She was busy threading cubes of meat onto skewers. Her fingers seemed to work to a hypnotic rhythm. She pierced the meat with a sudden stab and then tore the skewer slowly through it. When she speared the next piece of meat, watery blood dribbled over her fingers. Neil felt nauseous. His heartbeat seemed to thump out the seconds. He coughed and she turned round.

'Well then, what d'you think of the room?' She wiped her hands on a dish cloth and came into the living room.

'If you want it, I'll need a month's rent in advance, eighty pounds.' She wiped her brow and turned the fire off. Neil felt a surge of panic. He hadn't brought any money with him. Flustered he looked in his wallet. He had twenty pounds in notes and a few pounds in loose change.

'I've only got twenty pounds on me.' He smiled apologetically. 'Could I leave it as a deposit and bring the rest tomorrow?'

'OK,' she said. 'If you leave a deposit I'll keep the room for you till tomorrow, but if you're not here by dinner time I'll have to let it go to the next person who comes along.' Neil nodded and carefully laid two crumpled ten pound notes on the table.

'Could I use your phone?' He asked. 'I want to call a taxi.' A taxi was an extravagance he couldn't afford, but he was feeling faint again and didn't think he was well enough to make it back to the hospital under his own steam.

'There isn't a phone,' she told him, 'I used to have a pay phone in the hall but the tenants kept trying to rob it so I had it taken out. Nearest phone box is a half a mile away back on the main road towards town.'

In the end Neil had got the bus back to the hospital. There had been no sign of Tracy or Katharine, and the staff had turned on the smiles and charm for the arrival of the afternoon visitors. Neil had settled himself amongst the row of patients staring vacantly at the day-time television and waited for time to pass.

CHAPTER FOURTEEN

So today Neil was taking the advance rent for the bedsit. He saw Marlborough Road on the left and got up to get off the bus. He waited on the edge of the kerb for a space in the speeding, seemingly never-ending traffic racing this way and that, like a shoal of darting fish. Eventually he got to the other side of the road, walked left for a few yards and then turned right into Sovereign Road. It was a long walk down the road to number one hundred and sixty-three. It was past mid-day by the time he got to the house and he was breathing hard, and had a splitting head-ache. The house was shabby looking, a mess of crumbling brickwork and peeling paint. The front garden was paved with uneven concrete slabs and high weeds and thistles grew up between the cracks. A discarded broken toilet nestled amongst the wild plants. Neil walked through the open gate mottled black and brown with flaking paint and rust, pushed through the unlocked front door and rapped on Betty's sitting room door.

There was no sound from Betty's flat. Neil rapped on the door again, harder. He rubbed his knuckles and waited. Perhaps she was in the kitchen and couldn't hear him he thought. He dithered, uncertain whether he should just walk in. He decided he had to see her to make sure he didn't lose the room. He opened the door to her flat. It felt stiff and heavy. Then he realised the draught excluder was jamming it. He tried kicking it out of the way but it had wedged under the door. He squeezed through the gap.

The heat was overpowering. The curtains were closed and the room was lit only by the fierce orange glow of the fire. The room looked dirty and menacing in the fiery light. As his eyes grew accustomed to the gloom, he could see someone's arm hanging over the edge of the chair.

'Mrs. Redmond I've brought the rest of your money' he said in the direction of the chair. There was no reply. He went over to her but her eyes were closed and she was motionless. It felt as though the heater had been on full blast for hours. The heat felt as though it was searing his throat and lungs, and he spluttered with a spasm of coughing that reached so deep into his lungs he retched. He reached down and turned the heater off. He felt light-headed and dizzy. He was gasping for air and was afraid that if he didn't stop coughing he would actually be sick. He lurched into the kitchen and filled the nearest mug with water. His first sips were spluttered back up, but as he managed to keep some of the water down, the coughing subsided a little although he could still feel the irritation in his lungs. Hoping vehemently that Mrs. Redmond wouldn't object he opened the back door and let himself sink down on the step. Brittle

November air buffeted him. He gasped it in. Then the darkness inside his head absorbed his consciousness, and he lapsed into a world of fast action dreams.

When his awareness returned his memory didn't immediately follow. He stared at the backyard mystified as to where he was and what he was doing there. Slowly though, memories of the past couple of hours became present in his mind and sorted themselves into place. He swung round expecting to see Mrs. Redmond keeping a wary eye on him, but the kitchen was empty. Perhaps unable to rouse him, she had retreated to the warmth of the sitting room, he thought. He went back inside. She seemed to be asleep. He wondered why she was still in her nightclothes.

'Mrs. Redmond' he said loudly. He took her arm and shook it lightly. She showed no sign of waking up. He stared at her. For one heart-stopping moment he thought she might be dead but her rosy complexion belied that. Perhaps she had fainted from the heat he thought. He bent over her. 'Mrs. Redmond wake up,' he said as loudly as he could without shouting. He took hold of her arm and shook it vigorously. She slumped heavily against him. She felt like a dead weight. He put both hands on her arm and pushed her back in her chair. Her head lolled awkwardly on her shoulder. Neil was sweating heavily and feeling panicky. She needed a doctor he thought. She had said the nearest phone was half a mile down the road. He could try the neighbours but if they were out it would cause further delay. He tried to remember what they had been taught in first aid classes at the mental health day centre. He pushed back her lank hair hanging over her puffy face. He couldn't bring himself to stick his fingers in her mouth to check she hadn't swallowed her tongue. He had to do something. Air, air. It was an aimless thought but it suddenly made a connection. He stumbled across the room and pulled back the curtain. He fumbled with the window latch and pushed hard. It wouldn't budge. Then he saw the window locks. He felt along the sill for a key but there was nothing. He turned and went to the sitting room door. He tried pushing and pulling it this way and that but it remained tightly wedged on the draught excluder. He couldn't get it open more than a foot. There was nothing else for it. He had to get her out of this suffocating heat and into the fresh air.

He went back into the sitting room, grabbed Betty under the arms and started hauling her towards the kitchen. It was like trying to lift several hundred weights of coal. He could just barely keep her head and shoulders off the ground; the rest of her body dragged along the floor. Her slippers came off one after the other. He figured if he could just get her outside the crisp air would revive her. He pulled her through the kitchen door and across the kitchen floor to the back door. He manoeuvred her head and shoulders through the back door when his knee buckled. She slipped from his grasp, and with a resounding crack her head slammed onto the back door step. He reached down for her and froze. Her jaw hung open.

'Oh my god' he said out loud. 'Oh my god.' His voice was high-pitched and croaking. 'Oh shit!' Indecision swamped him. He stood on the doorstep shaking. He felt for her pulse like they'd been taught in the first aid classes. He wasn't sure if

he could feel anything or not. He had to get help. He stepped over her, stumbled through the kitchen, squeezed through the sitting room door and pounded on the door of the bedsit opposite. The silence was torture. He banged on the door again with the side of his fist.

'It's an emergency!' He yelled. The side of his hand stung. He started up the stairs. His hand slid on the dusty bannister. He used his other hand to knock on the door on the next landing. He thought he heard the sound of movement in the room but then it fell quiet. He heard laughter but couldn't tell which direction it was coming from. Maybe it was inside his head. He hauled himself up the next flight of stairs. He ignored the stinging of his hands and thumped the door with both fists. 'Help, it's an emergency,' he shouted breathlessly. He heard someone turn the latch and the door swung open. The man looking at him was in his thirties; his muscles bulged under his t-shirt and he looked fierce. There was something familiar about his face but Neil couldn't quite place it and he hadn't time to think about it now.

'What d'you want?' Terry snarled. Neil gasped for breath and forced words out disjointedly.

'There's a woman, hurt, downstairs.' He couldn't think what else to say. He was trembling and put his head against the door frame to steady himself. He flinched as Terry shrugged his shoulders with disdain.

'What d'you want me to do about it?' Terry asked. Neil tried not to cry.

'Help, please help,' he pleaded. Terry looked down at him smirking.

'Jesus, you're pathetic,' he sniggered. He shouldered Neil out of the way and strode with deliberate casualness down the stairs. Neil scuttled after him. Terry stopped in the ground floor hallway and spread his arms wide. 'Where is she?' He demanded. Neil jerked his arm up waving it in the direction of Betty's partly open door. 'In there?' Terry barked. Neil nodded his head.

'Mm' was the only noise he could articulate. Terry tried to push the door open but it was still stuck on the draught excluder.

'What the fuck, is she behind the door?' Terry asked. Neil shook his head. Terry slipped through the gap and with an exasperated grunt wrenched the draught excluder from under the door. The material tore and some of the filling fell out. 'Jesus, it's like a fucking sauna in here,' Terry said. As Terry looked round the empty room Neil edged in after him. 'Where is the old cow then?' Terry asked. Neil nervously beckoned Terry to follow him. Even though he knew what he would find it still shocked Neil to see Betty lying outside the back door. He had half been expecting that it had been some dreadful hallucination and she wouldn't be there. The reality of seeing her lying there unmoving made him feel intensely sick. Terry pushed him to one side and nudged Betty with his foot tentatively. She didn't stir.

He crouched down beside her and lifted her shoulder so he could see her face. He looked at her waxy, impassive features and slack jaw, and the colour drained from his face. 'What happened?' He rasped.

'I dropped her' Neil stammered in a barely audible whisper. Neil was going to explain exactly what had happened but was silenced by Terry's glare.

'You've fucking killed her' Terry shouted. Hysteria and panic jolted through Neil like an electric shock.

'No,' he whimpered. He tried again to explain but the words wouldn't come to him.

'You have, you stupid bastard, you've fucking killed her,' Terry raged. He stood up, his face contorted, his body tense and menacing. Something was prodding at Neil's memory. All his alarm bells were ringing. He just didn't know how to deal with this situation. He had to get away. He had to get away somewhere where he could clear his head. He had to get away. It was all he could think of. He backed out of the kitchen, through the sitting room and out the front door. For a few seconds he bent over gulping in air and then he ran blindly up the road.

Terry stood staring at Betty's body for a few moments uncertain what to do. Then he walked back through the kitchen intending to go to the phone box down the road and ring for an ambulance. As he entered the sitting room though Betty's hand-bag caught his eye hanging on the armchair in front of the fire. He paused for a moment and then went over and closed the sitting room door. He went back to the armchair and started rifling through Betty's bag. There was forty pounds in cash in her purse which he stuffed in his pocket, but there was nothing else that was any good to him. He looked round the room carefully. There was a fourteen inch colour television. He could just about manage to carry that, Video recorder, no problem. The stereo was going to be too heavy for him to carry out in one piece and it would take too long to disconnect the sections. Nah, he'd leave that but he'd noticed the microwave in the kitchen, he'd have that. He'd changed his mind about calling an ambulance. Instead he went outside to his car. He drove round to the cul-de-sac that ran along the back of the houses, and parked outside Betty's backyard. He left the car door wide open, flipped both the seats forward and went through the gate into the backyard.

He grabbed Betty and pulled her clear of the back door. As he struggled to move her he backed into the dustbin which fell over sideways, and the lid clattered on the paving. Terry shrunk down beside the wall. Opposite the back of the house was a row of garages which screened him from view, but he was afraid the noise would bring the next door neighbours to their windows. He stayed huddled against the wall for several minutes. Finally he stood up and glanced quickly at the bedroom windows of the houses next door. There was no sign of anyone. Within a few minutes he had put the television and video on the back seat of his car and the microwave on the front passenger seat. He jumped in the driver's seat and quickly pulled away.

Dreams Of Death

CHAPTER FIFTEEN

Escape. It repeated itself in Neil's head. Escapescapescape. The urgency of it quelled the panic threatening to overwhelm him. He moved with robotic determination. One foot pounding after the other as each bent arm mechanically punched the air in front of him. The shock of his feet hitting the ground stung the soles of his feet and reverberated through the muscles of his legs. His stomach ached from the strain of the slight left to right, right to left swing of his upper body as he ran. Through his jacket he could feel the warmth of under arm sweat. Sweat tickled itching as it dribbled down his chest and back gluing his shirt to his skin. The roots of his hair were wet with sweat despite the brittle cold air. Sweat hot on his forehead had turned dully cold by the time it dripped from his chin.

Ahead of him two twenty something young women gabbled at each other by the kerb, mouths and hands animated. Waves of coarse accents and profane language floated to him from the distance. The taller of the women rocked a pushchair to and fro across the pavement; rudely oblivious to the obstruction she was causing. A baby lay asleep in the pushchair it's body muffled by blankets, its tiny face pinched, eyes tight shut asleep. Neil couldn't slow down. He tried to call out a warning but his voice was mute. As he collided with the pushchair the woman screamed. Neil stumbled but kept going. He knew he should stop, but he couldn't he was so scared.

'Fucking lunatic bastard' the woman shouted after him. After that Neil had no memory of how he got back to the hospital Back on the ward he couldn't believe how appalling life had become in the space of a day. Yesterday he had been worried about coping, but he had been looking forward to regaining his independence. To being able to make a cup of tea when he was thirsty, instead of having to wait for the tea trolley every two hours on the ward, and not being able to get a cup of tea all night when he couldn't sleep. He'd also been looking forward to cooking for himself. Not that he was a gourmet chef or anything, but he could rustle up a tasty meal when he felt well enough, not like the cardboard tasting stuff they served up in here. He had lost over a stone in weight since he had been in hospital because he couldn't stomach most of the meals. He relied on the toast they made for supper to fill him up. He'd been tentatively thinking about getting himself a little allotment. The doctors wanted him to go to a day-centre but he didn't want any of it. He wasn't interested in the dead-end activities. If you had done one anxiety management, assertiveness or relaxation course, you'd done them all. The alternative was 'employment.' Counting nails into boxes for five pounds a week, he found it demeaning.

He wanted to do something constructive, something productive. It was hard to know what exactly, but he knew it definitely wasn't what they had on offer. He thought an allotment might be the answer. He could see himself in the sunshine, a gentle breeze ruffling his hair, listening to music on his Walkman surrounded by the satisfying sight of green shoots, growing and changing every day, and looking forward to the sense of achievement of cooking his home-grown vegetables. His only worry was that when he got ill he wouldn't be able to maintain the plot. If other allotment holders complained to the council that it was getting overgrown it could be taken off him. He hadn't managed to figure a way around that. He didn't want another failure to add to the list. But right now all that was a pipe-dream anyway.

Since he'd got back at the hospital his mental state had been worsening. The voices were telling him he was a killer. The newspaper headlines he'd seen in town now seemed to hold a personal message for him. 'Schizo slays' the voices chorused. 'Lunatic let loose. You killed her, you're a killer!' The psychological anguish was unbearable, like razor blades being drawn across every nerve in his body. He believed human life was precious. His whole life he had tried not to hurt anyone. Now he felt he was to blame for someone's death. It was unendurable. By now he had only a hazy recollection of what had happened at Betty's. The more he thought about it the more jumbled up it seemed to get. He knew he had caused her death. The accusation that he had killed her kept resounding through his head. He couldn't live with himself if he had killed, not even if it was accidental, and by now that man would have reported to the police that he killed her. They would be searching for him even now.

His illness had made him timorous. He wouldn't be able to stand up for himself. If the police pushed him, he would just agree with whatever they wanted him to say. He couldn't cope with pressure and what could he say in his own defence, when it was true that he'd killed her? Neil knew he wouldn't last long in prison. He was passive. He would be bullied mercilessly. He had heard from other patients the things that happened to mental patients in prison. It would kill him.

He knew the police would be after him. That man would have told them. That man knew; he knew the truth. That man…Neil had that tip of the tongue feeling. There was something about that man he was trying to remember. He had recognised him. They had met before. He was sure of it. Then he saw Terry's face, magnified in front of him, his mouth moving in slow motion as it bellowed the words 'You've fucking killed her,' again and again. Then in a petrifying moment of realisation it dawned on him where he had seen

Terry before. He was the man who had mugged him in the hostel. The man who had threatened to slit his throat. Neil's stomach somersaulted. What if the man came after him? He might want revenge for Betty's death. There was no telling what he would do.

It seemed impossible to escape this catastrophe. No-one would believe it had been an accident when he was a mental patient. There was a witness saying Neil had killed Betty, a violent man who could be looking for him this very minute. He felt intensely that there was only one solution open to him – suicide. He felt too confused and apathetic to think it out right now, but first thing in the morning he would find a way to kill himself.

That night he couldn't sleep. He felt agitated. He didn't know what to do with himself. He sat on the edge of his bed rocking backwards and forwards, but it didn't bring him the usual relief from tension. In total despair he went to talk to the night nurses. The nurses were sitting at a table near the entrance to the ward. A couple of the women were knitting. Another woman and a young male nurse were playing cards. One of the female nurses looked up at Neil and scowled as he approached them. Neil sat down at the table with them.

'We don't encourage patients to sit at the nurses' station,' the scowling nurse said. Neil stood up.

'I've got to talk to someone,' he said desperately. The nurse ostentatiously consulted her watch.

'It's three in the morning, you should be asleep. If you don't sleep now, you'll sleep during the day.'

'I can't sleep. I feel terribly ill. I feel suicidal,' Neil begged.

'Well what do you want me to do about it? She asked nonchalantly. Tell your doctor about it at ward round tomorrow. Now John, she indicated the young male nurse, will see you back to bed.' John gripped Neil's arm with both hands and escorted him back to the dormitory. Back in his bed Neil continued to try to grapple with his quandary. He lay writhing and muffling his sobs in his pillow until the day shift came on duty.

Dreams Of Death

CHAPTER SIXTEEN

Neil had just dropped off to sleep when a nurse woke him for the doctor's ward round. Desolately he meekly trudged into the doctor's office. Dr. Johnson looked up from his notes as Neil came in.

'How are you feeling Neil?' He asked. Neil seized the moment. He couldn't get the nurses to listen to him. The psychiatrist was his last chance. He poured out his story, talking rapidly. His recollection of what had happened at Betty Redmond's was muddled and hazy, and his account came out rambling and incoherent. Neil realised he was gabbling, but couldn't think how to word it more succinctly so the doctor would take him seriously.

'I think I've killed someone and I'm suicidal,' he reiterated in conclusion hoping the emphasis on these clear facts at least would convey to the doctor the desperation of the situation. Dr. Johnson's gaze was steady. His expression was kind, but inscrutable. He looked remarkably composed Neil thought. He supposed the doctor must have heard it all with his experience.

'So, a woman has died and you feel responsible for her death?' You've had thoughts like this before haven't you?' The doctor asked calmly. Neil shook his head no. 'I think you have Neil.' The doctor spent several minutes re-reading through some of Neil's medical notes again. 'Yes. There have been times when you've felt that people blamed you for your baby daughter's death? Times when you yourself were convinced you caused her death, and since then there have been others episodes. Cases you read about in the newspapers, or saw on the television when you were absolutely certain you were responsible for the deaths of complete strangers.' Tears of frustration welled in Neil's eyes. 'And people have talked to you about that haven't they? Your previous doctors, hospital nurses and your community psychiatric nurse perhaps, hmm. They've talked to you about your baby's inquest and its finding that your daughter died of cot death. That you tried to resuscitate your daughter, that you did everything possible to save her.'

'It's not my daughter this time. It's not my daughter's death I feel responsible for.'

'What makes you feel responsible for this woman's death Neil?' Neil was too distraught to answer.

'Look you've had suicidal thoughts before haven't you, and not acted on them? Feeling like it and doing it are two very different things. How could you challenge your negative thoughts?' Neil continued to sob. The doctor leaned forward. 'Neil, to my knowledge you aren't responsible for anyone's death. Not your daughter's and not anyone else. I think you're ill. Your thoughts aren't real. They have become distorted and confused. I don't really want to increase your medication at this stage. You've been quite stable on your current dose for some time now, and you get very apathetic on a higher dose. Try to think of ways to challenge these thought or distract yourself from them.'

'I didn't mean to kill her,' Neil answered, 'but the man who mugged me said I killed her and the voices say I killed her. I'm so afraid.' His voice was getting shrill.

'You've been mugged?' Dr. Johnson couldn't quite disguise the note of impatience in his voice.

'Yes, well no, not yesterday, a long time ago.' Neil realised his story was just sounding more and more fabricated and fell silent again. Dr. Johnson looked at his watch.

'I wish I could talk to you about this for longer Neil, but I have other patients waiting to see me. Challenge the thoughts or distract yourself from them' he repeated. 'Try talking to the nurses if it's difficult to do on your own. You can go now.' Neil sat steadfastly in his chair. His life depended on this. He scoured his mind for a way of conveying the reality of his fears to the doctor, but he couldn't think of anything he hadn't already said.

'Doctor, you've got to help me' Neil demanded. Dr. Johnson's patience failed him.

'Neil, I've got other patients to see,' he said curtly. 'You've got a severe, and enduring mental illness that will get worse as you get older, there isn't anything more we can do for you.' The doctor nodded at the male nurse who was taking notes. The nurse took Neil by both arms, pulled him up from his seat and marched him out of the office.

On the ward Neil cried out loud. His mind was in turmoil. He sat, huddled in a chair in a corner of the day room. The noise of the ward faded into silence. His vision blacked out and he felt as though he was suspended in space. He strained to hear something but everything was quiet. He strained his eyes to see something, but all he could see was a blanket of darkness. He clenched his hands to feel something but there was no answering sensation. Abruptly out of the darkness flashed a vivid, magnified image of Betty's face with its sagging jaw. He could feel again the moment her weight slipped from his grasp. He clutched at the air vainly for the reassurance of her bulk safe in his hands again, but there was no substance for him to hold. He could see her falling and the crack as her head hit the step. The scene replayed itself over and over again.

***

Katharine Baines sat watching him. Perturbed by his obvious distress she went to the office where Glenda, Neil's keyworker was doing some paperwork.

'Can I talk to you for a minute? Katharine asked her. 'It's Neil Soames. I'm worried about him. I think he's getting more ill. He seems very distressed, anguished. Can you do something?' Glenda frowned at the interruption.

'He's putting it on because he doesn't want to be discharged' she said, and dismissed Katharine with a glare. Katharine wanted to say something more and tried to think what more she could say to validate her concern, but she couldn't think of anything and didn't have the confidence to argue. She decided that when Neil came out of his trance she would try to talk to him, and see if there was anything she could do to help.

It was nearly an hour later before Neil came out of his reverie. The silent black screen in front of him suddenly vanished to be replaced by the normal sights and sounds of the ward. Katharine went and sat next to him.

'How did it go with the doctor?' She asked and then cursed herself. It was clear it hadn't gone well.

'He didn't listen' Neil cried, and responding to Katharine's concern recounted his tale. Katharine listened patiently but couldn't really make head or tail of what he was saying. The only bit she grasped was that he thought he'd killed a woman. She didn't believe for a moment that he had killed anyone, but she didn't know how to reassure him.

'What woman, when, where?' She asked trying to make sense of his thoughts. Neil took a deep breath and tried to tell her the facts again as clearly as he could. She was afraid she might be intensifying his delusion by making him talk about it, and phrased her words carefully.

'Exactly how did she die?' Katharine asked. Her voice was shaking but Neil didn't notice. Someone was listening to him at last, taking him seriously. He tried to think how Betty had died but it wasn't clear to him, it hadn't ever been clear to him. He pictured the scene, him and the other man standing over Betty's corpse, the other man snarling that Neil had fucking killed her.

'I tried to help but I killed her,' Neil whispered. Katharine felt panic. She couldn't handle this. She had met him many times through the mental health system over the years and she knew he wasn't aggressive. She liked him, but she didn't know how to deal with him now.

'Excuse me, I've got to make a phone-call,' she said and got up and left. She felt guilty just leaving him. His suffering was patent, and he had stood up for her in the past, but she had no idea how to help him and she had troubles of her own. She went and sat on her bed in the dormitory. She was trembling. An image came into her mind of low-rise buildings silhouetted, monolithic against a bright, moonlit sky. There was a terrific bang, a noise like a thunderclap followed by a low rumble. The sky filled with orange flames. There was screaming. People were running. Some of them were on fire. She saw herself dashing frantically towards the shattered, blazing cadet base screaming for her son. She buried her head in her hands.

***

On the doctor's instructions the nurses kept Neil confined to the ward for the rest of the day, because of his suicidal thoughts. He hadn't slept that night, and had got up more determined than ever that he would kill himself as soon as he could get off the ward. He fell asleep on his bed as the day staff arrived. He had missed breakfast and dinner by the time he woke up, so after slipping past the nurses he went to the volunteer run coffee bar downstairs. He had a pot of tea and a tuna roll.
He didn't have any appetite, and had to force the food down but he thought he should line his stomach. It was important to his plan that he wasn't sick later.

He walked the ten minutes to the local shops. He was too early. It was only one-forty-five in the afternoon, and the shops were closed from one till two for dinner. Neil began pacing slowly up and down in front of the shops to try to keep warm. Did he kill her? Didn't he kill her? The question reverberated in his mind. It occurred to him there was a way to find the answer. If he leapt as far as he could and landed on a crack between the paving slabs it meant he had killed her. A leap that landed clean on a paving slab, without touching the cracks meant he didn't kill her. He closed his eyes, summoned all his energy and leapt. He landed on a crack. He shrieked with despair. Was it true? Maybe he hadn't been concentrating on that jump and it didn't count. He didn't want it to count. He puzzled over the problem and decided that it would be the third jump that would give him the true answer. Whatever happened on his third jump would be final. He leapt again and landed cleanly on a paving slab. He gulped and leapt for his third jump. He would be guilty if he landed on a crack, innocent if he landed on the slab. He landed on the slab. Sweet Jesus thank you he muttered, but after a couple of minutes of jubilation he began shaking his head. It was no good. He had cheated, changed the goal posts. He had to know the truth one way or another for certain. One more jump, the next one would decide it conclusively. He jumped and landed on a crack. He couldn't bear it. He jumped again. After three jumps he'd lost track of the results and had to start again. He jumped again and landed on a slab, but was off balance and took a step back that landed on a crack.

        'What did that count as? What did that count as?' He was shouting. He tried to calm himself. The pavement had rapidly cleared of people, as he bounded backwards and forwards over the pavement like an arthritic gazelle. Girls in the office above the shops were watching out of the window and giggling. Some teenagers had stopped to watch.

'Fucking nutter!' The boys yelled.

'He's doolally. You're a loony!' Their girlfriends shrieked. Neil sank to the ground and lay flat out exhausted. He still didn't have the answer as to whether he was guilty or innocent.

A few minutes after two o'clock an assistant unlocked the front door of the pharmacy. She turned over the card hanging in the door from Closed to Open. Neil heard the door unlock. He gave her a few minutes to settle in then went inside. A whoosh of warm air embraced him. He walked slowly round the stands, toiletries, shampoos, perfumes, make-up, and baby food. Then he saw the medicines. He stood in front of the shelves scanning the rows of cold remedies, cough medicines, laxatives and vitamin supplements. His search stopped when he got to the pain relief tablets. Anadin, ibuprofen, hedex, paracetamol, the names went on. He wasn't quite sure what he was looking for. He'd tried quite a few things in the past. You learnt from your mistakes. The only one he was sure you could kill yourself with was paracetamol. He picked up a small plastic bottle of twenty-five tablets, and read the warning on the side: Do not exceed the stated dose – an overdose is dangerous medical attention should be sought immediately. That was what he was looking for. He toyed with the idea of buying two bottles. He wanted to make sure he was taking enough. He was fairly certain twenty-five would do the job, and he didn't want to alert the suspicions of the sales assistant. He settled on buying one bottle and went up to the counter to pay.

When he came out of the pharmacy, he went straight into the grocery shop next door. He bought a litre carton of orange juice then went and looked at their pain killers. He shifted from one foot to the other. He was having doubts. Was twenty-five definitely enough? He had made unsuccessful suicide attempts before and he didn't want to go through that experience again. He bought more paracetamol and then made his way back to the hospital. He didn't go in the main entrance but followed the path that went round the back of the hospital. Out of sight of anyone he sat down; popped the first tablet in his mouth swallowed it down with a swig of orange juice, and mulled over his plan.

Neil knew it took a long time for the effects of a paracetamol overdose to show. He figured by the time there were any signs it would be night time, and he would be safely tucked up in bed where nobody would notice anything was wrong. He was a bit vague as to the deadline for administering the antidote. He thought from conversations he'd had with other patients that twelve hours after ingestion was probably the maximum time for the antidote to work. That meant by two-thirty in the morning his fate would be sealed. Even if the staff realized something was wrong at getting up time it would be too late. By that time the physical damage would be irrevocable and whatever they did he would die.

He swallowed another tablet and leant his head back against the wall. For the first time in a long while he was smiling, he felt wonderfully calm. He couldn't remember when he had last felt this relaxed and at ease. His mind felt startlingly rational and clear. The tranquility cocooned him. He didn't even feel the cold, and with each tablet he swallowed the serenity deepened. When he had finished taking all the tablets he returned to the ward, and settled down in front of the television. A couple of the other patients were watching snooker. Neil wasn't interested in the game, but it was a way to pass the time uninterrupted, and to keep himself inconspicuous while the tablets did their work.

CHAPTER SEVENTEEN

At two-thirty in the afternoon on the same day; Elizabeth Lingwood
was sitting at her window again. She was looking at the white van
which was back again and parked down the road. She was trying to
decide whether to call the police. She had felt a bit embarrassed the
last time she called them. She was sure they thought she had
overreacted, and that she was just some sad old woman who only
called them out for a bit of company, but she was keeping an eye on
the van just in case. After arguing with herself a bit longer she lifted
the telephone receiver.

Inside the white van Mick Hughes and Terry Fields were
keeping watch on their target house.

'Promise me Terry, promise me you didn't kill the old girl,'
Mick appealed to Terry.

'I've told you haven't I? I've told you again and again what
happened. I never laid a finger on her.'

'The police were ok right? When they called at your bedsit
for a witness statement, they were fooled? You don't think they were
suspicious of you?'

'They were putty in my hands. I told them I'd been out
drinking with you that dinner time and they were happy as sand-
boys. A nice tight alibi makes their lives easier.'

'Oh great!' So not only am I handling your stolen goods I'm
providing you with a false alibi. That's perverting the course of
justice. If this goes pear-shaped I'm going to be in deep, deep shit.
And that's only the law, if Lyndsay finds her Mum's stuff in our
garage she'll go ape-shit,' Mick persisted. 'She won't stand for it.
You've got to admit your story doesn't sound likely. I wish I could
believe you. This is too much Terry. We've been mates a long time. I
covered for you on that aggravated burglary and did extra time for it,
and I've put up with you slagging down Lyndsay all these years, but
if you topped Lyndsay's Mum I won't cover for you. A bit of thieving's
one thing but I won't condone murder.'

'I'm not asking you to,' Terry shouted, 'I never touched her.
I've told you what happened. I really don't give a shit whether you
believe me or not, but just fucking shut up about it will you. I don't
want to hear another word about it.'

'You can have all the cash from this job,' Mick told him, 'just
so long as you go away. I want you away from me and my family.
You could go to the continent. You should be able to get some work
in the building trade over there.'

'And what about the cash from Betty's stuff?'

'Christ, are you never bloody satisfied? There's not a hell's
chance of getting a fence to take stuff that hot. The woman did die!
As soon as I can move it without Lyndsay seeing I'm throwing it all in
the canal.'

They both looked up as the family who lived in the house drove off.

'Now. Let's get it done,' Terry commanded. They had taken the jewellery from the upstairs and were loading a computer from downstairs into their van when
the police arrived. The house was at the end of a cul-de-sac and there was nowhere for Mick and Terry to run.

***

As Mick and Terry were arrested for burglary; Katherine Baines was on her way into the town centre. She was sick of sitting on the ward, she wasn't expecting any visitors and she was feeling a bit better, so she had decided to get some fresh air and a change of scene. It was the first time she had been off hospital grounds since she had been admitted. She hadn't planned what she was going to do in town, but it was too cold for window shopping so she decided to go to the library.

Katharine browsed first at the Medicine and Health Section. A nurse had called her up to the medicine trolley this morning and handed her a tablet. When she had asked the nurse what it was he had said fluoxetine. That meant absolutely nothing to her and she wanted to know what she was taking. She pulled the British National Formulary off the shelf and looked up fluoxetine. It was an anti-depressant, otherwise known as Prozac and it had a long list of side-effects. She almost wished she hadn't looked. She picked out another book on Coping with Depression, and sat down at an empty table to skim through the pages.

After half an hour her concentration started to feel strained. She looked at her watch. She still had time to spare before she needed to be back at the hospital in time for tea, and she wanted to put off going back out into the cold, but she was feeling tired. She closed the book on depression and got up to leave.

As she passed the enquiry desk the Newspaper and Periodicals stands caught her eye. She had taken several more steps before a sudden thought brought her to a halt. She half turned back and then turned forward to leave again. She was too tired to read anymore, she couldn't be bothered, but if she went back to the hospital now it would still leave an hour before tea, and she would only be bored and more than likely start ruminating over her negative thoughts again. She turned back once more and walked over to the newspaper stands.

It was only a small thing. It wouldn't take long and Neil had been a good friend to her over the years, she could do this for him. Neil had said he killed the woman on Thursday. She chose Thursday's local paper from the stand and began reading the headings. 'Woman Raped and Murdered,' jumped out at her and her heart started to pound. She hated reading things like this they made her paranoid and gave her nightmares. She carried on scanning the paper headlines. By the time she got to the end of the paper her head was aching, and the print was dancing in front of her eyes. There was nothing in the paper that sounded remotely like what she was looking for. She closed the paper; folded it and placed it back on the shelf. This was a fool's errand she told herself, but now she had started it, it would nag at her if she didn't finish it. She fetched Friday's paper to the table and started to read.

On an inside page there was an article headlined 'Woman's Death Riddle.' Katharine read on. It said police had launched an enquiry after the body of fifty-two year old Betty Redmond of Sovereign Road had been found in her backyard, by her
daughter and son-in-law yesterday. Her death was suspicious. Cash and a number of other items were missing from her flat in a house she let as bedsits. Police believed Mrs. Redmond had been killed in a burglary that went wrong. Cause of death couldn't be established until they had the results of a post-mortem. The police were appealing for any information from the public. Katharine put the paper down and let the article sink in. Burglary? Neil hadn't said anything about a burglary but all the other details matched what Neil had told her.

It couldn't possibly be coincidence. She made herself read the article over again slowly. After reading it a second time she sat back in her chair; closed her eyes and took some deep breaths. She hadn't seriously expected to find anything in the paper. This, was amazingly good news. As she opened her eyes the artificial lights made her blink. The surroundings were their ever unchanging shape. A couple of people were browsing through the music section. A man at the next table was reading the Daily Telegraph. There was the low drone of hushed voices. In this tranquil context the verification of Neil's revelations seemed absurdly unreal. With a suppressed sense of excitement she went to get Saturday's paper. She had to know if there was any more news about the death, but Saturday's paper wasn't there.

Katharine hurried over to the photocopier to make a copy of the article about Betty Redmond's death. She had no ten pence in her purse, and as she was getting some from the change machine an announcement came over the public address system.

'Your attention please, the library will be closing in five minutes, the library will close in five minutes, please make your way to the exit.' Katharine checked her watch. She hadn't realised the time. She tried one photocopier but it was colour copies only at a pound a time. She queued up behind the man using the only other photocopier. The minutes ticked by. She thought about leaving it and coming back on Monday to get the copy, but she wanted to have the article to show Neil. She might need it to convince him he hadn't done anything bad. It was virtually five o'clock now and the man in front of her showed no sign of finishing. Katharine glanced around. The library was practically empty. The public address system started up again. 'The library is now closed. Please make your way to the exit.'

'Sod it,' Katharine muttered under her breath. She took another quick look round the library. Nobody was looking at her. She deftly folded her coat over her arm covering the newspaper, and walked smartly to the exit, her face crimson with guilt.

Nobody called out to stop her, and she ran down the library steps and outside where the cold air met her burning cheeks like a smack in the face. She crossed the precinct to the nearest paper shop and bought Saturday's local paper. She scanned the headlines while she was in the shop, but could see anything that might give further information on Betty Redmond's death. It felt like such an anticlimax. She wished she had some information that could completely quell Neil's fears. She rang the ward from the kiosk outside the shop to explain that she had missed the bus so
would stay in town for tea. She felt excited in a very agitated sort of way, and she needed to calm down before she went back to the hospital. The nurse who answered her call said that as long as she was back before the staff change-over at nine it was fine. She walked to 'Jones,' a restaurant/bar where you could get dinner for less than a fiver, ordered a meal and a camomile tea and sat down. She liked this place. You got a real social mix, from business people to students and pensioners. She idly leafed through the Saturday's paper while she waited for her meal.

If she hadn't looked through the paper a second time she would have missed it. She hadn't realised it was what she was looking for the first time through, but there under the headline of 'Mystery Death Caused by Killer Fumes' was an account of how Betty Redmond had died. The article reported that the police were now in possession of the post mortem results on Betty Redmond, and that she had died from carbon monoxide poisoning which had since been traced to a faulty gas fire in her living room. Gas officials had released a statement saying that the fire had not been serviced for years. Katharine cried tears of relief. Although they had never seen each other as a regular thing she really liked Neil. This was such good news; the best news. This would surely convince him. In black and white he was exonerated. She couldn't wait to tell him.

By the time she had eaten her meal, waited for the bus and travelled the hour back to the hospital it was seven o'clock when Katharine arrived back on the ward. She looked in the day room for Neil but there was no sign of him. She asked one of the men sitting in front of the television if he knew where Neil was, and he said he thought Neil was having a bath. Katharine put the newspapers in the drawer by her bed for safe keeping and went to the smoking room for a cigarette.

Neil was having a quick bath. He wanted to be fresh and clean for when they found him. He was having moments when the finality of what he was doing frightened him a little, but as soon as he considered the prospect of going on living with the memory of what he had done his resolve to die was strengthened once more. He got out of the bath and dried himself and put his pyjamas on. He had begun feeling queasy in the last hour. He was worried he would collapse or throw up or something in front of the nurses alerting them that something was wrong with him, so he had decided to make an early night of it and go to bed. It was only sevenish, but as long as you didn't cause trouble or fall down at their feet the nurses didn't notice much what you did.

The nurse brought the tea trolley into the day room just after eight o'clock. Katharine collected her cup of tea and sat waiting for Neil to come for his. By quarter past eight most of the patients had been to the tea trolley and the tea urn was empty, but there was no sign of Neil. She went and checked the bathrooms but the doors of both of them were open and there was no-one in them. She asked the man in the day room again if he had seen Neil. He said no impatiently, but the man sitting next to him said he had seen Neil getting into bed nearly an hour ago.

Katharine went to the men's dormitory and hovered at the doorway. She couldn't see Neil. She was eager to tell him the fantastic news, but female patients weren't allowed in the men's dormitory and she didn't want to get a tongue-lashing from the nurses. She decided to leave it till the next day. She was disappointed and now the excitement of sharing the news with Neil was on hold she felt worn out. She decided she would have a relaxing soak in the bath. She went straight to bed herself afterwards and within half an hour she was asleep.

At one o'clock in the early hours of the morning Katharine was woken by a vivid dream. She couldn't remember what it had been about, but it had left her mind racing and she couldn't get back to sleep. She tossed and turned until two o'clock, and then got up and went to the smoking room for a cigarette. She had just sat down when she saw Neil walk past the door on his way back to bed after going to the toilet.

'Neil,' she called quietly. He turned towards her. 'Neil, can I talk to you for a minute?' He hesitated but came into the smoking room and sat next to her. She clasped his hand excitedly. 'Neil, you didn't kill that woman. I can prove it to you. Will you wait here a couple of seconds? I've got something important to show you, it's in my dormitory.' Neil nodded. He didn't really want to talk to her and he wanted to get back to bed, his head was feeling muzzy, and he was afraid he would be sick but Katharine's enthusiasm was persuasive. He could wait for a few seconds.

Katharine hurried to the dormitory. She didn't feel at all sure he would wait. The night nurses glared at her when she came back out of the dormitory carrying the newspapers, and she was afraid they would order her back to bed. She scurried resolutely back to the smoking room. She was relieved to see Neil still sitting there, but she noticed that he looked sickly and pale. She opened the papers at the relevant pages and passed them to Neil. He stared at them vacantly.

'It's about the woman you told me about, the one who died,' she exhorted. Neil looked startled. 'Do you remember telling me about a woman who died?' She asked gently.

'The woman I murdered,' Neil corrected her.

'No, no you didn't kill her, it's in the paper, read it,' she implored. Neil gazed at the papers. At first she didn't think he was actually reading, but then she saw that his eyes were moving almost imperceptibly along the lines of print. She waited tensely. Neil's hands went slack and the papers slid to the floor. He let out a soft low moan. Sweat glistened on his face. He opened and closed his mouth as though suffocating.

Katharine clutched his hand alarmed. His skin was cold and clammy.

'It's all right Neil. You didn't kill anyone. Did you read it? It says in the paper she died of poisonous fumes.'

'I didn't kill her. I didn't kill anyone.' Neil echoed Katharine's words repetitively, while tears cascaded down his face. He looked at Katharine. 'Are you sure? Are you sure it's right? It's not a mistake?'

'I'm absolutely certain,' Katharine stated happily.

'Can I, can I keep them? Neil asked, picking up the papers.

'Of course,' Katharine smiled.

Neil folded the papers up and tucked them under his arm. He sat in silence with his head bowed for a few moments, and then said quietly

'I've taken an overdose.' The smile slipped from Katharine's face.

'What have you taken? How long ago?' Katharine questioned with dismay.

'Umm, early afternoon,' Neil mumbled. Katharine raced to the nurses' station.

'Come quickly. It's Neil Soames. He has taken an overdose.' The Charge Nurse marched to the smoking room with her.

'What did you take, how many and when? The nurse asked Neil peremptorily. Once she had the details she scurried back to the nurses' station.

'Call an ambulance!' She ordered.

Dreams Of Death

CHAPTER EIGHTEEN

Three months after Elizabeth Lingwood witnessed the burglary, she was singing to herself as she sat at her dining room table to write to Sarah, Neil's ex-wife. She had sent Sarah a Christmas card, but hadn't written her a proper letter since the autumn and she had a lot of news to tell her.

> Dear Sarah, she wrote. I am so pleased to hear that you have found lasting contentment with your second husband. After all the grief and pain you went through in the past no one deserves to be happy more than you.
>
> I too have some happiness after such a long while, and it has sprung from a most unfortunate incident. Last November I witnessed two men attempting to burgle my neighbours' house opposite. I called the police and the burglars were apprehended at the scene. My neighbours' possessions were safely returned to them so no permanent damage was done.
>
> However my neighbours', whom I had not met before due to my housebound condition, came across to me that evening to thank me for being a good neighbour and calling the police. They were ever so nice and we got chatting, and the upshot was that they asked me if I would give some coaching to their daughter who is struggling with her English exam work. I agreed and she has been coming to my house for a couple of hours a week ever since, but that is not all. My neighbours told other parents their daughter was getting extra tutoring at a reasonable cost, and other parents have contacted me asking if their children can come to me for help. Word has spread, and the headmistress from my old school now recommends me to parents of children who are having difficulty with their English.
>
> It is so exciting to be working again. It doesn't make masses of money but it all helps and that is not the point. My self-esteem is so much higher now I feel useful again. I can't believe that I spent so many years just sitting here, when I could have done this all along, but I lost so much confidence after Dad died I didn't feel like trying to do anything, and I was so focussed on overcoming my fear of leaving the house it never occurred to me to have the children come to me.

On top of this I have found that with this change in circumstances my faith has returned. I feel so much strength and joy now. I got in touch with the old church we used to go to and explained that I am not able to leave the house, and they now hold home church meetings at my house on a regular basis.

Well, that is all my news for now so I will say good-bye. Wishing you continued peace and contentment.
Much love,
Elizabeth

***

After arresting Mick Hughes and Terry Fields at the scene of the burglary the police had searched both their homes including Mick's garage. Lyndsay had identified her mother's stolen possessions stored inside, and forensics showed Mick and Terry's fingerprints all over them. There was no point for Mick and Terry in trying to deny their guilt. In a last ditch effort to save his marriage, and maybe get a shorter prison term, Mick told the police about Terry beating up the householder they had burgled years earlier who had been left disabled. Terry told the police about Neil but they knew Betty's death had been an accident, and they knew it was Terry who had stolen her things. They weren't really interested in spending investigative time trying to find someone who didn't appear to have committed any crime, and who sounded suspiciously like a figment Terry had thought up to try to confuse the issues and off-load some of the blame.

Three months after the burglary Lyndsay was making her first visit to Mick in prison. She had been eating better and had put on a few pounds since Mick had been jailed. The extra weight suited her and she knew it. She was looking and feeling much more healthy and confident. She had left the children at home. She had decided to make some serious changes in her life, and she wanted to be able to talk to Mick without the children running round.

Mick didn't show any surprise when Lyndsay told him she wanted a legal separation. After all she had warned him if he went to prison again their marriage would be finished. The fact that he had helped Terry with the theft of things taken from her own mother sealed the decision. Mick begged, cajoled and argued to try and get her to change her mind, but this time she wouldn't be persuaded. She told him that she had made friends with an older woman from the

Offenders' Relatives Association, and that the woman was going to help her find childcare so that she could go to college.

'I'm bright Mick. I did well at school. I'm going to do a Nursery Nursing course. I've got four babes of my own, I know a bit about it. I'm young. I've had no youth. I don't want to go on living like this. I want a better life for myself and for the kids,' she told him.

***

Katharine Baines was discharged from the hospital without knowing what happened to Neil. She had asked the nurses if they had any news of him the day after the ambulance had taken him to the general hospital for treatment, but all the nurses could tell her was that he had been transferred to a specialist liver unit, and was being given the antidote but it could go either way. She had tried contacting the liver unit, but had been told that patient information was confidential and could only be given to relatives.

She didn't know where Neil had been living before his last admission to hospital, and although he had once asked she had always been too paranoid to give him her own address. It seemed like she would never know what happened to him, and that she had lost her occasional friend forever. Katharine felt wretched and cried endlessly. What had happened to Neil was so cruel and unfair. Eventually though, she decided for her son's sake she had to try to not dwell on it, and focus her mind on more positive things.

Katharine had still felt ill when she left the hospital, but a few weeks after her discharge they had changed her medication, and it really seemed to lead to an improvement in her condition. Three months after her discharge she was trying to take steps to make a new life for herself. She didn't feel able to return to work yet, but she had applied to do an Open University course. They would give her credit for the study she had done previously at university. It would take years but she had hopes that if she paced herself carefully she might yet get a degree. She was also keeping her eyes and ears open for something lighter and more recreational that she might do until her study started. Today she was going for an appointment to try something new. She approached the small anonymous building feeling a bit nervous. She was met inside by a woman who showed her into the office.

'My name is Eloise, I am the professional artist helping out with this project,' the woman explained. 'The "Art Room" is a small project led by mental health service users to provide opportunities for people with mental health problems to participate in art, in an informal and encouraging environment. And you think you would like to give it a try?'

'Yes. I mean I'm not actually any good at art, and I haven't done any since I left school but I always enjoyed art lessons. I'm looking for ways to fill my time that won't be too stressful and where I can get out and meet people, so yes, I would like to give it a try.'

'Well, we would be very pleased to have you join us. Would you like me to show you around?' They left the office and Eloise opened the door of the art room. 'Let me introduce you to one of our volunteers. This is Katharine. She's a newcomer to the project,' Eloise said to the man sitting painting at the easel. Katharine did a double take as the man turned towards her.

'Hello Katharine,' he said warmly.

'Hello again Neil,' she said, and they both smiled.

Lynda Anning

ACKNOWLEDGEMENTS

I would like to express my heartfelt thanks to my friend Sarah Housden who was my first reader, for her constructive criticism and encouragement. My thanks also to my son, Peter, for his ideas, encouragement and computing help; and my thanks to Luke Kesterton for permission to use his photo for the front cover image.

Dreams Of Death

www.ingramcontent.com/pod-product-compliance
Lightning Source LLC
Chambersburg PA
CBHW031215270326
41931CB00006B/566